MW00575527

BEHIND THE BBQ

Recipes, Cocktails, & Tall Tales

DICKEY'S BARBECUE PIT®
est. 1941

ROLAND DICKEY, JR., ROLAND DICKEY, SR., & LAURA REA DICKEY

with *Jerry Murray & Chef Phil Butler*

Dickey's Barbecue Pit is an American family-owned barbecue restaurant chain based in Dallas, Texas, and is a subsidiary of Dickey's Capital Group. Since Travis Dickey established the restaurant in 1941, it has become the largest barbecue franchise in the world.

Special thanks to the following individuals for their contributions to the development of this book:

Roland Dickey, Sr., Author

Roland Dickey, Jr., Author

Laura Rea Dickey, Author and Editor

Aaron Brewer, Production Assistant

Jamie Henretta, Creative Director

Chef Phil Butler, Recipe Development and Preparation

Lauren Lumbley, Dickey's Managing Editor

Betsy Orton, Assistant Editor

Jerry Murray, Copy Editor and Assistant Editor

Scott Nelson, Rusty Hill, Brianna Dickson, Photography

4514 Cole Avenue, Dallas, TX 75205
972-248-9899
dickeys.com

Copyright © 2021 Dickey's Barbecue Pit
All rights reserved. No part of this book may be reproduced or transmitted in any form or by any means, electronic or mechanical, including photocopying or recording, or by any information retrieval system, without the written permission of the copyright holder.

ISBN: 978-0-87197-609-3
Library of Congress Control Number: 2021915030
Printed in USA
10 9 8 7 6 5 4 3 2 1

Behind the BBQ: Recipes, Cocktails, & Tall Tales was edited, designed, and manufactured by Favorite Recipes Press in collaboration with Dickey's Barbecue Pit. Favorite Recipes Press works with top chefs, food and appliance manufacturers, restaurants and resorts, health organizations, Junior Leagues, and nonprofit organizations to create award-winning cookbooks and other food-related products. Favorite Recipes Press is an imprint of Southwestern Publishing House, Inc., 2451 Atrium Way, Nashville, Tennessee 37214. Southwestern Publishing House is a wholly owned subsidiary of Southwestern Family of Companies, Nashville, Tennessee.

Christopher G. Capen, President,
    Southwestern Publishing House

Sheila Thomas, Publisher,
    Favorite Recipes Press

Mary Velgos, Art Director

Kristin Connelly, Managing Editor

Linda Brock, Editor

Rhonda Brock, Proofreader

frpbooks.com | 800-358-0560

Kim –
Happy BBQ!
Best
Laura Dickey
2022

DEDICATION

Barbecue lovers. Pit Masters. Big Yellow Cup collectors.
This book is dedicated to all the folks who have made
Dickey's Barbecue what it is today. Your passion for
Legit. Texas. Barbecue.™ has transformed our little barbecue
joint into the largest barbecue brand in the world.

To our Dickey's Team, thank you for your partnership and
all that you do every day to serve our slow-smoked barbecue
to as many folks as we can. Let's keep the fire going.

CONTENTS

INTRODUCTION

No one imagined Dickey's Barbecue Pit would grow beyond a single restaurant, much less become an international restaurant brand. Today, eighty years after opening, we are the largest barbecue restaurant brand in the world. I can look back and see the faces of hundreds of people who have helped us achieve this distinction—from everyone at our Home Office to suppliers, manufacturers, and most importantly, our restaurant franchise owners and guests. We have the privilege of serving Legit Texas Barbecue to guests all across America—and now around the globe.

Inside this book, you'll find many of the same recipes I grew up enjoying, others I've created, and many more from our extended Dickey's family of Pit Masters, patrons, and lifelong friends.

Dickey's Barbecue started with a single restaurant opened by my dad. The tradition of the family business continued with my wife, Maurine, and my sons, Roland, Jr., and Cullen. Just as I did with my father, my sons worked the restaurant as soon as they could handle a potato peeler. As they grew up and pursued their own careers, Roland dedicated

Roland, Jr., Cullen, and Roland Dickey, Sr.

his wits and talents to the restaurant business, while Cullen has become a successful commercial real estate broker.

As I grew Dickey's over the years, I wasn't sure what would become of the barbecue business. I knew if the business was to succeed long term, any member of the family who wanted to join the company needed to first work successfully for another restaurant group.

After Roland, Jr., had worked a few years learning the ropes with a national, full-service restaurant corporation, my brother and I asked him to come back to Dickey's. In 1999, he started off as a general manager and ran our only full-service location in Albuquerque, New Mexico, for two years. Then, he worked his way up through the company to vice president and was named CEO of Dickey's Barbecue Restaurants, Inc., in 2011. He has since gone on to create additional related companies, manufacturing sauces and spices, creating custom metal fabrication for restaurants, and developing hospitality technology—all under the Dickey's Capital Group umbrella. Roland currently serves as the CEO of Dickey's Capital Group.

Roland, Jr., at original Dickey's in 2010

At the end of this cookbook, you'll read the epilogue, written by my daughter-in-law Laura Rea Dickey, who currently serves as CEO of Dickey's Barbecue Restaurants, Inc., in addition to Spark Hospitality Technology, Inc. She and Roland married in 2006. They run the Dickey's companies much like Dad and Mom did and like Maurine and I did. It truly is a family business.

It's an amazing thing to look back over my life and realize my path has taken me from Pit Master behind the block to pitch man in front of the cameras to traveling the country opening restaurants, and now back full circle to what matters most: eating good food, being surrounded by family and friends, and telling and hearing a lot of Texas tall tales about the good old days.

I asked my daughter-in-law why we wanted to publish a second Dickey's Barbecue cookbook. After all, I wrote *Mr. Dickey's Barbecue Cookbook* ten years ago, and it's pretty great if I do say so myself.

Back row: Roland, Jr., Roland's wife, Laura, Cullen's wife, Allison, and Cullen Dickey
Front row: Roland Dickey, Sr., Cullen and Allison's son, Warren, and Maurine Dickey

(Pulitzer is in the mail, I'm sure.) She reminded me that we've done a lot in the past decade, and our story continues. Plus, so many great folks have helped build the brand, and what better way to celebrate eighty years than to share their stories and recipes and recognize how much they've helped us to serve Legit Texas Barbecue?

I sincerely hope you enjoy this journey through *Behind the BBQ: Recipes, Cocktails, & Tall Tales* from Dickey's Barbecue Pit. It truly has been my pleasure to serve you.

Roland Dickey, Sr.

Roland Dickey, Sr., celebrating with guests

DICKEY'S BARBECUE PIT:
THE BIGGEST "LITTLE BARBECUE JOINT" IN THE WORLD

Family owned and operated since 1941, each Dickey's restaurant serves authentic Texas-style barbecue that is smoked over a real hickory-wood pit onsite in each location every day. No shortcuts. No substitutions. No exceptions.

1941

The original Dickey's Barbecue in 1946; Travis Dickey with Elizabeth and T. D. (for Travis Dickey, Jr.)

Certified Pit Masters chop, slice, or "grab, squish, and tickle" each of Dickey's eight signature meats to order for guests. With twelve sides, secret original barbecue sauce, and the iconic Big Yellow Cups of Dr Pepper® or Miss Ollie's Sweet Tea, it is easy to understand how Dickey's is both that authentic, family-owned barbecue joint around the corner and the largest barbecue restaurant brand in the world.

What started as a single barbecue stand in Dallas, Texas, eighty years ago has been passed down through three generations and now extends to over 600 restaurants worldwide. The Dickey family is serving folks in forty-six states and introducing authentic Texas-style barbecue globally with locations in the United Arab Emirates, Singapore, Japan, Australia, Pakistan, and Brazil.

"Most folks are shocked to realize how large we are and that's a great thing," says Roland Dickey, Jr., CEO of Dickey's Capital Group. "We want to keep that authentic family feel. We always want to stay true to our roots but evolve where we need to keep guests happy. We serve many of our traditional recipes from three generations ago. And we've stuck with the motto 'if you wouldn't serve it to your mama, don't serve it.' Now, from Destin, Florida, to Dubai, you can order Dickey's full menu online and have it delivered straight to your doorstep."

Along with the food, authenticity and humor are at the heart of the Dickey's Barbecue experience. "My dad would never have imagined this. I didn't

imagine it when I took over the original location from him in the sixties," says Roland Dickey, Sr., Original Pit Master. "He needed to support my mom and our family, so he opened up a barbecue stand. When he passed suddenly, I needed to keep supporting my mom and my own wife."

There really were no intentional plans of grandeur. The Dickeys were truly in the business of serving great barbecue to other families, so they could support their own family. As Roland told his own sons when they each got married: "The secret to a happy life is a happy marriage; and the secret to a happy marriage is to keep the cash coming and offer to do the cookin'."

There are many tall tales, Texas truisms, and secret family recipes to share as Dickey's enters its eighth decade of smoking brisket, ribs, and burnt ends.

"When people ask about Dickey's, I explain we're in-the-food-and-the-folks business. We charge for the barbecue, but the hospitality and tall tales are free," says Laura Rea Dickey, CEO of Dickey's Barbecue Restaurants, Inc. "When I was little Laura, I never dreamed my career would leave me smelling like barbecue every day, but I wouldn't change it. Aside from the food, the best part of my job, and Dickey's,

Roland Dickey, Sr.

is the people. I hope our cookbook captures that. I love sharing a little bit of our family's secret sauce and shenanigans with others."

This collection of recipes is gathered from the Dickey's Barbecue family at large. These are the best recipes from folks who officially have the last name Dickey and the folks that have earned the Dickey's moniker by helping build the business, run the restaurants, and oversee the pits throughout the years. In these pages, you'll find plenty of tips to upgrade your home 'cue. You'll also learn how to prepare the perfect cocktail, shortcut your way to gourmet, and discover what's in the sauce. This cookbook has great barbecue recipes but also includes what we serve beyond barbecue in our own homes. It's a little peek behind the barbecue, and a thank you to the folks that make Dickey's what it is today.

"We do barbecue, not rocket science, around here. It's a great way to make a living—playing with fire, selling brisket, and sharing laughs. So, we have to serve the best barbecue to folks and do a great job. I don't want to get fired. I'm not cut out for anything else," says Roland Dickey, Sr., Original Pit Master.

From our table and our family to yours, thank you. Let's eat.

Dickey family outside of the original location in 2021

A BRIEF HISTORY OF THE DICKEY'S BARBECUE STORY THAT'S PROBABLY, MOSTLY ACCURATE

As you can imagine, Dickey's was quite a bit different in 1941 than it is today. Believe it or not, the original restaurant (known as Central for being located on Central Expressway in Dallas, Texas) opened and sold only pit-smoked brisket and ham sandwiches for 50 cents each; fries or chips for 20 cents; beer and sodas in bottles, and pints and half pints of milk for 10 to 20 cents. You could have a whole meal for less than a dollar! Like a lot of barbecue joints back then, it was quite smoky inside, and not just from the pit. The lunch-hour folks used this time as their designated smoke break, too. Dickey's closed at 5:30 p.m. on weekdays and 4:30 p.m. on Saturdays, and they were closed on Sundays. Dickey's met the needs of their guests and in return became their go-to lunchtime sandwich spot.

Travis Dickey, Sr., was not only a great father and husband, but also he had a great sense of humor that connected with Dickey's guests. He loved to talk to the customers and tell jokes as they came through the serving line. And Miss Ollie Rich, Travis's wife, also worked in the restaurant, right alongside her husband—often seen behind the cash register. In later years, she kept the books for the business. The Dickeys grew up working class and rarely had enough money (or time) to take vacations, but they always had food and a roof over their heads. Travis Dickey, Sr., and Ollie Rich had three children, Elizabeth Mills, the late T. D. (Travis Dickey, Jr.), and Roland Dickey. T. D. was the first of the family to attend high school and went on to study at Southern Methodist University (SMU) in Dallas, Texas, which quickly became a family affair as Elizabeth and Roland both followed in T. D.'s footsteps at SMU.

Roland Dickey, Sr., Miss Ollie Rich, and T. D. enjoying a bite to eat

Longtime guests waiting for lunch outside the restaurant in 1941

Dickey's original location today

Elizabeth Mills' wedding day, with her father, Travis Dickey, Sr.

Elizabeth is known to be the best cook in the Dickey family. Oftentimes, Roland teased their mother that she couldn't cook, especially throughout Dickey's early years on television commercials. In reality, their mother was a great cook. Roland Dickey proclaims himself as a self-taught cook, but the truth of the matter is he learned from his mom and sister.

1994

Dickey's Owner/Operator Bob Rusnak and Colorado Pit Crew with Laura Rea

1967

Roland Dickey, Sr., outside Richardson, Texas, location

"My dad opened the barbecue stand, and my brother and I turned Dickey's into a few restaurants. Then I started the catering business and the franchising business," says Roland Dickey, Sr., Original Pit Master. "By 1994, we had opened thirteen Dickey's Barbecue Pit restaurants. It was then that I decided it was time to evolve and grow our family business with partners and franchises."

Dickey's began franchising to bring Texas barbecue to everyone and grow the brand worldwide. The first two franchisees, the Smith family and the Azul family, are still Dickey's restaurant Owner/Operators today.

Over the years, people have questioned how Dickey's stays authentic. "Simple," says Roland Dickey, Jr., CEO of Dickey's Capital Group. "We still prepare things the way my grandfather did. We work with suppliers to get the best cuts of meat. We use our secret seasoning to dry rub our meats, then we load them into real barbecue pits. Every restaurant has a real wood-burning barbecue pit. You can always smell the smoke from the parking lot."

With expanding the brand in mind, Dickey's launched a proprietary training program, Barbecue University, a three-week course that certifies folks in every aspect of the barbecue business. The program certifies Pit Crews and Pit Masters to carry out our purpose—to serve as many folks as we can our Legit Texas Barbecue every day. Barbecue University includes specialized courses so team members can continue to develop their own career paths and skill sets. Dickey's has evolved over the years, adding to the menu, adding locations nationwide, and expanding outside of Texas to Colorado in 1998.

Roland Dickey, Sr., with sons, Cullen and Roland, Jr.

"My sons, Roland, Jr., and Cullen, both gave the restaurant business a try. I told them both that if they wanted to join the family business, they first had to work for someone else successfully for at least three years," says Roland Dickey, Sr., Original Pit Master. "After SMU, Roland, Jr., went to work for the El Chico Mexican Restaurant company as a Kitchen Manager and worked his way up. After some time in the food business, Cullen decided his passion was actually real estate. He chose to pursue a career in commercial real estate. Cullen has been very successful in opening his own real estate office and still handles many of Dickey's property deals today."

After Roland, Jr., had experience under his belt, T. D. suggested bringing him back to Dickey's. By the mid to late 90s, the franchise business was starting

Roland, Jr., accepting Ernst and Young 2015 Entrepreneur of the Year award

to expand, and business was quickly evolving, especially with computers running just about everything. The company had a total of sixty-eight restaurants in six states at the time. In 1999, Roland, Jr., was asked to open and run a family-owned Dickey's, in Albuquerque, New Mexico, for a year. He then moved to California for six months to support new restaurants opening in that state and next moved to Colorado for another six months to support the operations in that growing market. After earning his operations experience in the field, he came back to the Dallas Home Office to become Vice President of Operations. He excelled in this position and was named President and then CEO of Dickey's Barbecue Restaurants, Inc., in 2006. Roland, Jr., led the company from 90 restaurants when he took the helm to 600 restaurants to date.

In 2003, Roland met Laura Rea, a graduate of Texas Christian University (TCU) in Fort Worth, Texas. Laura had worked for several marketing agencies and specialized in —of all things—

Roland, Jr., and Laura Rea **2004**

hospitality and restaurant marketing and technology development. She moved to Dallas to join The Point Group and ended up joining the Dickey family as well. In 2006, Roland, Jr., married Laura. In 2009, Laura was drafted into service for the family business. "It was the 2008 recession, and that was a challenging time for everyone. It was all hands on deck, so I jumped in to set up community marketing and 'deal with the dang computers.' Then, they kept adding to my job," laughs Laura Rea Dickey, CEO of Dickey's Barbecue

Restaurants, Inc. "I'm literally married to work, and strangely, that works for us."

Together, Roland, Jr., and Laura now run all six of the Dickey's companies, with Roland as the CEO of Dickey's Capital Group and Laura as CEO of Dickey's Barbecue Restaurants, Inc. "We divide and conquer. We are literally opposites, so what one can't do, the other can," says Roland Dickey, Jr. "People ask which one of us is in charge, which makes me laugh. Laura explains it's whoever makes the coffee first that morning."

"I am so happy to know that the future of the company is in their very capable hands," says Roland Dickey, Sr.

Roland Dickey, Sr., with Roland, Jr., and Laura Rea

Under their leadership, the littlest barbecue joint in the world has skyrocketed over the years to more than 600 restaurants and expanded into the Middle East in 2018, followed by steady growth in Singapore, Japan, Australia, Pakistan, and Brazil. The Dickey's brand has also vertically integrated to better support all areas of the business, opening a sauce and spice manufacturing company, a hospitality technology company, a craft sausage company, and even a direct-to-guest online food company, Barbecue at Home by Dickey's.

The barbecue is important, but it's the people that matter.

Dickey's has been fortunate to have many long-standing team members and even some folks who have joined the company as second-generation team members. Randy Hubbard is one of those people. Randy's father and Roland Dickey, Sr., would drive an old box truck to catering events, and at one point, the U-joint fell apart and left them stranded on the side of the road.

"We called Randy's father 'Chef.' I said, 'Chef, if you can fix this truck, you have a job for life.'" says Roland Dickey, Sr., Original Pit Master. "Surprisingly enough, he fixed the truck and had a job for life." After his father had a stroke and could only work part-time, Randy

Randy Hubbard and long-term employee Angel Cortez working the block

came on and started working for the company and still works with Dickey's today. He's an ordained minister, and in fact, he preached at the late T. D.'s funeral. "I saw Randy the other day, and I asked him, 'Randy, can you be sure to outlive me, so you can preach at my funeral?'" says Roland Dickey, Sr.

"When will that be," Randy asked me with a grin on his face, "so I can plan ahead?"

DOING WELL & GOOD—THE DICKEY FOUNDATION

Being involved in the community has always been a part of Dickey's history. Whether it was sponsoring little league teams, donating barbecue to the neighborhood schools, or hosting community gatherings in the dining room, part of the barbecue business has always been building relationships and supporting the community. "We first formalized our commitment to being a good neighbor with our community involvement program in 2009," explains Laura Rea Dickey, "Our purpose is threefold. First, serve our great barbecue to as many folks as we can every day. Second, expand the family with great folks, partners, and guests by staying true to our authentic barbecue experience. Third, do both well and good in the communities in which we do business. We have to be successful, and then we must give back to our communities as thanks for our success."

This community involvement and civic stewardship evolved into The Dickey Foundation in 2016. The Dickey Foundation was created and is enthusiastically led by Maurine Dickey, wife of Roland Dickey, Sr., specifically to support first responders—local law

enforcement, firefighters, emergency medical professionals, and their families. The foundation is national, yet the support is intensely local—benefiting first responders who put their lives on the line every day, serving the public. "I've always believed in public service. I started out in social work and then led children's social services for the state of Texas. I served on the Parkland Hospital Board and even as a Dallas County Commissioner," says Maurine Dickey, Dickey's Foundation Chairwoman. "Giving back matters. I've seen the difference it makes. It's the glue of a community. It was a natural next step for our family to set up a nonprofit foundation dedicated to giving back. I am very proud to lead that effort."

Dickey's female leadership team with the Pink Big Yellow Cup

2016

Dickey Foundation Executive Director Betsy Orton with Maurine Dickey and Rusk County Sheriff Johnwayne Valdez

To date, The Dickey Foundation has donated over 100,000 pulled pork sandwiches through our first responder support packs. The original First Responder Tribute Cup sold more than 844,000 cups, raising more than $111,000 for The Dickey Foundation. Dickey's Barbecue Pit also joined the fight against breast cancer with the debut of its first limited-edition Pink Big Yellow Cup. The Dickey Foundation raised $45,000 and has used the funds raised from the collectible Pink Big Yellow Cup to provide mammograms and other breast-cancer detection, treatment, and services for local first responders.

SURVIVING TO THRIVE AGAIN—THE PANDEMIC THAT COULD HAVE TAKEN DOWN THE RESTAURANT INDUSTRY

Everyone remembers exactly where they were during big moments. One of those collective big moments is certainly the COVID-19 pandemic. Devastating and surreal, the "coronavirus" went from late-night talk show fodder to painful reality for all in March 2020. Many people lost so much. Many folks suffered, and our prayers are still with them. The pandemic bears mentioning in Dickey's history because one of the immediate ramifications during its onset was the shuttering of restaurant dining rooms across the country.

What does that mean for a restaurant company, or even the industry? Dickey's Barbecue Pit has the distinction of being the oldest, continuously operating restaurant in Dallas, Texas. Since October 1941, the original location on Central Expressway has never shuttered its doors, changed ownership, or changed locations.

The original pit had been fired up every day for eighty years. "And 'it's not going down on our watch' is exactly what I said to my husband, Roland, when he called me to discuss options after the national quarantine news broke," says Laura Rea Dickey, CEO of Dickey's Barbecue Restaurants, Inc. "I was in Florida, visiting Owner/Operators. He was in Texas, working at the Home Office. We had to come up with a plan.

Chef Phil Butler preparing drinks to-go while dining rooms were closed due to the pandemic

2020

Dickey's Owner/Operator Wendy Williams created her own to-go table to meet the needs of guests.

It was a defining moment, but there was actually no question. "We had to find a way to keep serving, to be there for our communities, and to keep our folks employed," says Laura Rea Dickey. Dickey's employs over 169 employees directly and over 6,000 indirectly through restaurant locations. Those figures don't even include all the folks employed through Dickey's additional restaurant-support companies. Understanding the supply chain, the Dickey's team knew grocery stores wouldn't be able to sustain consumers' food demands for very long without help from restaurants. So, the company shifted resources and focused all of their business online via delivery or curbside pickup. Dickey's could serve guests safely with small groups working in each restaurant. The team knew folks needed to eat, and they needed hope, purpose, and help so that's what Dickey's provided through slow-smoked barbecue.

Dickey's Owner/Operator Tom Eggerud feeding Minnesota first responders

To provide help to Dickey's Owner/Operators, they cut royalties by 50 percent (not abated but cut them) for fourteen weeks to give restaurant Owner/Operators more cash flow. "We called in every favor we had with every supplier and partner that we had strong relationships with and ensured food would get to the restaurants," says Laura Rea Dickey. "We battled supply shortages. We navigated truck driver shortages. Our employees stepped up to the plate in the most selfless ways possible." Laura also held remote webinars every day for a month to talk candidly about challenges, choices, and perseverance and to personally connect with each restaurant.

"Our Home Office team took a voluntary pay cut so we didn't have to cut hourly jobs in the restaurants," says Roland Dickey, Jr., CEO of Dickey's Capital Group. "Everyone rose to the occasion, and we were able to ride the tide until it turned again."

Several things helped Dickey's continue serving— to survive and then thrive again. "We didn't raise prices," says Laura Rea Dickey. "Instead, we made our dine-in-only Kids Eat Free on Sundays available online." Dickey's knew everyone needed help. They added more Family Pack options in smaller sizes, as well as added basic groceries for purchase. Laura took any television interview available to spread the word nationally that Dickey's was open and ready to safely serve guests by meeting their comfort level. Most importantly, Dickey's also focused on giving back to first responders by implementing special First Responder Support Packs. Guests could purchase and donate sandwiches online, the Dickey family would match each free sandwich donated, and local restaurant owners donated the free delivery to local hospitals, police stations, and fire stations.

Dickey's made it through. In fact, sales increased double digits after the initial shock of March 2020. Initially, more than 10,000 sandwiches were donated to first responders. Against all odds, Dickey's actually opened new restaurants during the pandemic. The

Top: Laura Rea national remote segment with Neil Cavuto on Fox News television station
Above: Chef Phil Butler set up for a remote food segment

company also realized that you must learn from every challenge, so the team went to work on adding revenue streams and making improvements.

Coming off the 2008 United States economic recession, Roland, Jr., and Laura realized what changes needed to take place to ensure the brand endured. Roland went to work on shrinking the footprint and increasing per-square-foot profitability. Laura went to work on design and technology infrastructure. "We opened the kitchens so folks could see the real wood-burning pits," says Laura Rea Dickey. "We also put a ten-year strategy in place to evolve technology, which led to us creating our own online ordering system, Point of Sale, and such."

Roland also led research and culinary development efforts and created a world-class culinary team. The company went to work on finding the best possible folks to expand the team. "All of these investments and lessons from 2008 and 2009 are what prepared Dickey's to handle the unimaginable challenge of 2020," says Roland Dickey, Jr. "It's the tough days you learn from and lean on when you have to lead through the next challenge. The pandemic could have ended everything; instead, we chose to fight, we survived, we banded together, and we served until we thrived again."

In fact, Dickey's expanded in new ways because of the pandemic, starting with launching Barbecue at Home, Dickey's direct-to-consumer brand. Folks can order Dickey's one-of-a-kind barbecue products, savory sides, and subscription meat delivery boxes online from BarbecueAtHome.com. This brought barbecue and comfort food to folks' front door to smoke, grill, and cook whenever they wanted.

The Dickey Foundation with Maurine Dickey partnering with Dickey's Owner/ Operator Jeff Bass to feed every first responder in Garland, Texas

Similarly, Dickey's listened to guests and figured out how they could deliver what folks needed and wanted most. Dickey's Kielbasa Sausage has a cult following, and guests wanted more, so the company launched Dickey's Craft Sausage Company, offering over twenty types of handmade gourmet sausages direct to guests online. Dickey's also expanded their retail products in grocery stores, launching new barbecue sauces and spice rubs and adding flavors of barbecue beans across the country.

Finally, Dickey's has started opening three sister restaurants: Wing Boss (chicken wings and tenders), Big Deal Burger (burgers and fries), and Trailer Birds (Nashville hot chicken).

"I love our business. I loved going to work with my dad when I was a kid. I love that he always included me and taught me so much," says Roland, Jr. "I hope to live up to his work ethic. I believe business is either growing or shrinking. There is no in-between, so we are always striving to build Dickey's to ensure our family business keeps growing and going."

So, that's the story of how a little barbecue joint in Dallas, Texas, became the biggest barbecue brand in the world. The Dickey's team ensures every location nationwide still feels like the original store in Dallas, Texas, and treats guests and partners like friends and family.

Since the dawn of time, man has been fascinated with fire—its power, warmth, and ability to transform food and lives. As a young boy, I remember cookouts in Wisconsin, with everything from fish boils to Korean beef cooked over cherry and birch flames. The power of fire and smoke entrances people, and for chefs, it's a lifelong passion to control and bend it to our will to create mouthwatering food that leaves our family, friends, and guests in awe and asking for seconds.

Barbecue is the epitome of balancing heat, smoke, and time . . . lots of time. Born from a need to turn inexpensive, tough cuts of meat palatable, barbecue has become a time-honored tradition and the source of more than a few heated arguments about the "best" style,

Chef Phil Butler

which is obviously Texas barbecue. While brisket is the reigning king of Texas barbecue, it is a heavily worked muscle that requires time, care, and attention to turn it into the work of art we call Legit Texas Barbecue. To be honest, my first few attempts at brisket produced mixed results because of the roller coaster of temperatures produced by my smoker's firebox. My weekends became consumed by experimenting with burning wood—changing the size, the schedule, and anything possible to give me the control that would produce competition-style barbecue I could be proud of.

Fast forward hundreds (actually thousands) of briskets later, I joined Dickey's Barbecue Restaurants, Inc. With its eighty years of tradition steeped in hickory smoke, I was thrilled to join the first family of barbecue. Each day, I have the opportunity to work with seasoned Pit Masters, who have spent decades honing their craft. And it truly is a craft—each pit is different and each brisket is different. Over the years I have learned so much from so many of our long-tenured team members, be it how a meat might need just a little more time on a specific pit or how they know exactly what their regular guest is going to order when they walk in the door.

Working with the Dickey family, our Owner/Operators, and our Pit Crews across the country to create this cookbook has been a dream come true. Bantering with Mr. Dickey, Sr., about barbecue and how we can tweak recipes while staying true to our roots has been invaluable. He shared some techniques, tricks, and family secrets, and I'm happy to share those with you now.

To kick things off, you need to prep and get stuff organized. Everything always tastes better when the spice has a chance to marinate into the protein you are planning on cooking. Whether you want a dry rub, oil marinade, liquid marinade, or cold butter marinade, they all round out a great piece of meat when you give it time to do their job . . . plan ahead.

Don't burn the house down. The grill is like your car, you must take care of it after driving. Clean out old grease from the bottom, brush the grates, empty the grease catch, scrape and brush the insides and lid. Try to drive that grill over and over without doing this, and it will leave you on the side of the road in a big fireball, possibly taking the patio and house with it.

The art of great barbecue starts with telling your neighbor you know what you're doing. Opinions on grilling should be kept on the other side of the fence. Turn your favorite tunes on the radio and tackle the 'cue. Just know that when you pass over a bite of the perfectly cooked steak to your neighbor, and they look back at you like "Damn, how did you get that flavor," you are on your way to mastering the backyard barbecue.

Rest and grab a beer. Once you remove anything from a grill or pit, make sure you let it rest! The texture will soften, juices will remain and not run out onto the cutting board, and flavors will balance out.

When it's time to enjoy, don't get fancy trying to bounce salt off your elbow onto the meat. Save the skills to slice the meat properly, always against the grain to maximize tenderness. Seasoning meats twice is always better. During the marination and prep process, a little salt should be added to help flavors move into the meat. But finishing with good-quality pink salt or sea salt flakes adds a bright burst of flavor, accenting the smoky grilling flavors.

At the end of the day, if this doesn't work out for you, there's probably a Dickey's Barbecue Pit nearby that would be happy to help you.

Chef Phil Butler

Chef Phil's outside Pit Master's kitchen

APPETIZERS & SHARES

TEXAS TWINKIE
KOLACHES

Prep Time: 3½ hours (plus 8 to 10 hours)   **Difficulty:** Medium to Hard   **Serves:** 6 to 12

INGREDIENTS

12 medium jalapeños peppers

4 ounces cream cheese, softened

2 ounces shredded sharp Cheddar cheese

1½ pounds smoked brisket, cooled and chopped

12 thin slices bacon

1 tablespoon Dickey's Rib Rub

⅓ cup water at 110 to 115 degrees

1 tablespoon active dry yeast

¼ cup plus 1 teaspoon sugar, divided

⅔ cup whole milk at 110 to 115 degrees

4 tablespoons unsalted butter, melted, divided

1 egg, beaten

1 teaspoon kosher salt

4 cups (about) all-purpose flour

Mustard or barbecue sauce, for serving

DIRECTIONS

Preheat the oven to 350 degrees. Slit the jalapeños vertically from top to bottom and make a crosscut directly under the stem, cutting only halfway through. Remove and discard the seeds and membranes. Arrange the jalapeños on a baking sheet. Bake for 10 minutes. Remove the jalapeños to a bowl of ice water to help remove the remaining seeds and to reduce spiciness; may omit this step. Pat the jalapeños dry with a paper towel.

Combine the cream cheese and Cheddar cheese in a bowl and mix well. Spread 1 tablespoon of the mixture in each jalapeño. Place about 2 ounces of the chopped brisket in each stuffed jalapeño and wrap with a slice of bacon. Sprinkle evenly with the Dickey's Rib Rub and arrange on a heatproof wire rack. Heat a smoker to 275 degrees or preheat a grill for indirect heat. Place the wire rack in the smoker or grill. Smoke for 45 minutes or until the bacon is rendered and browned. Let stand to cool. Chill for 8 to 10 hours.

Mix the water, yeast, and 1 teaspoon of the sugar in a small bowl. Let stand for 5 minutes. Combine the milk, 3 tablespoons of the butter, egg, remaining ¼ cup sugar, and salt in a mixing bowl and whisk until smooth. Add 1 cup of the flour and the yeast mixture and whisk until blended. Knead the dough with the dough hook attachment, adding remaining flour 2 tablespoons at a time until the dough pulls from the side of the bowl. Mix at medium-low

speed for 3 minutes. Shape the dough into a ball and coat with the remaining 1 tablespoon butter. Place in a greased bowl, cover with a clean towel, and let rise for 1½ hours or until doubled in bulk. Line a baking sheet with parchment paper. Punch down the dough and divide into 12 portions. Roll each portion into a 4x2½-inch rectangle. Wrap each stuffed jalapeño with dough and fold to enclose completely. Arrange 2 inches apart on the prepared baking sheet. Let rise in a warm place for 30 minutes.

Preheat the oven to 425 degrees. Bake for 10 to 12 minutes or until golden brown. Turn the oven off. Let the kolaches stand in the oven with the door halfway open for 3 to 4 minutes; the insides of the peppers will be about 145 degrees. Serve the kolaches with mustard or barbecue sauce.

NOTE *Someone asked if we were going to add a Texas Twinkie recipe to the book. There are a few recipes out there. But it got us thinking, what if we took two iconic Texas foods and wrapped them up: Texas Twinkie Kolaches.*

BRISKET
CHILI CHEESE FRIES

Prep Time: 30 minutes   **Difficulty:** Easy   **Serves:** 4

INGREDIENTS

16 ounces frozen French fries

1 cup shredded Cheddar cheese

2 cups Smoked Brisket Chili
(recipe, page 146) or favorite chili

DIRECTIONS

Preheat a grill, oven, or campfire. Spray a large sheet of heavy foil with nonstick cooking spray. Place the frozen French fries in the center of the foil and fold the foil to enclose. Cook for 15 to 20 minutes or until cooked through.

Spread the Cheddar cheese and Smoked Brisket Chili over the fries. Close the packet and cook until the chili is heated through and the cheese is melted. Remove from the heat and open the foil slightly. Let stand to cool for 2 to 3 minutes before serving in the foil packet.

Mr. Dickey's
JALAPEÑO, CHEDDAR, & BACON LOG

Prep Time: 20 minutes (plus 1 hour)   **Difficulty:** Easy   **Serves:** 8 to 10

INGREDIENTS

1 jalapeño pepper, stemmed and seeded

4 ounces Gouda cheese

8 ounces sharp Cheddar cheese

5 ounces cream cheese, softened

2 tablespoons heavy cream

1 tablespoon Dijon mustard

½ teaspoon Dickey's Beef Brisket Rub

8 ounces apple-smoked bacon, chopped and cooked

Chips, crackers, or sliced crisp bread, for serving

DIRECTIONS

Mince the jalapeño. Cut the Gouda cheese and Cheddar cheese into ½-inch pieces. Pulse the Gouda cheese and Cheddar cheese in a food processor until finely ground. Add the cream cheese, heavy cream, Dijon mustard, and Dickey's Beef Brisket Rub and process until smooth, scraping the bowl twice. Add the jalapeño and pulse to mix; do not overmix.

Spoon the cheese mixture onto a large piece of plastic wrap and shape into a log. Wrap the ends of the plastic wrap tightly and roll the log firmly. Chill for 1 hour.

Coat the cheese log completely with the bacon. Serve on a platter with chips, crackers, or sliced crisp bread.

NOTE

Three of life's culinary pleasures—jalapeños, cheddar, and bacon—come together in an appetizer that will disappear not long after serving to your guests.

66 Using Dickey's Beef Brisket Rub, this is no ordinary cheese log. Your taste buds will have to work overtime to sort out all the incredible flavors."

BACON & POBLANO- WRAPPED MEATBALLS

Prep Time: 25 to 30 minutes   **Difficulty:** Medium   **Serves:** 12 to 15

INGREDIENTS

4 or 5 (4- or 5-inch) poblano peppers

12 to 15 Italian-style meatballs

4 ounces Colby-Jack cheese,
cut into 12 to 15 cubes

12 to 15 slices bacon, at room temperature

4 teaspoons Chili Pork Rub
(recipe, page 78)

DIRECTIONS

Preheat a grill or oven to 275 to 300 degrees. Arrange the poblano peppers on the burner of a gas stove or on a wire rack in a grill. Char the peppers with a propane torch, turning to char evenly. Grill or bake for 5 minutes or until tender. Remove from the heat. Scrape the skins off the peppers using the edge of a knife; do not cut or rinse the peppers. Stem and seed the peppers. Cut each pepper into 3 long strips.

Heat the grill to 275 to 325 degrees. Stuff each meatball with a cube of the Colby-Jack cheese and reshape the meatballs, covering the cheese completely. Wrap a pepper strip around each meatball, pressing into the meatball and keeping the ends of the meatballs exposed. Wrap a slice of bacon around each pepper strip no more than two times and hold in place with a skewer; trim the bacon if too long. Season with the Chili Pork Rub. Arrange the meatballs bacon sides down over indirect heat. Grill until the bacon is rendered. Turn the meatballs over and grill until the bacon is rendered. Sear the meatballs over direct heat, turning once. Remove to a plate and serve immediately.

PORK BELLY
LOLLIPOPS

Prep Time: 4 hours (plus 8 to 10 hours)   **Difficulty:** Medium   **Serves:** 6 to 8

INGREDIENTS

4 pounds pork belly, skin removed

2 tablespoons Dickey's Rib Rub

1 teaspoon freshly ground black pepper

2 cups cranberry juice

1 cinnamon stick

1 (½-inch) ginger root, peeled and minced

1 cup Dickey's Original Barbecue Sauce

DIRECTIONS

Season the pork belly on both sides with the Dickey's Rib Rub and black pepper. Place in a pan and chill for 8 to 10 hours to marinate.

Heat a smoker to 225 degrees. Place the pork belly on the smoker rack and smoke for 3½ hours. Let stand to rest for 20 minutes.

Combine the cranberry juice, cinnamon stick, and ginger root in a small saucepan. Cook over medium heat until reduced by 75 percent, stirring occasionally. Add the Dickey's Original Barbecue Sauce. Bring to a simmer and turn off the heat.

Heat the smoker to 250 degrees. Cut the pork into 1-inch-wide strips. Cut crosswise into 1-inch pieces. Thread 4 to 5 pieces of the pork onto 6 to 8 skewers. Dip in the sauce and arrange on the smoker. Smoke for 20 to 30 minutes or until the sauce is partially caramelized. Arrange on a platter and serve.

NOTE

Surpassing all other food-on-a-stick favorites, Dickey's Rib Rub and Original Barbecue Sauce turn these pork belly treats into a tender, smoky, flavorful delicacy that'll put you in hog heaven. They are meant to be an appetizer, but guests will want them as the main course.

Laura Rea Dickey's
BRUNCH
BOARD

Prep Time: 30 to 40 minutes   **Difficulty:** Medium   **Serves:** 8 to 12

INGREDIENTS

1 cup mixed walnuts and pistachios

1 tablespoon honey

Salt to taste

6 slices wheat bread, toasted

Mashed avocado with lemon juice

Dickey's Everything Bagel Rub

Sliced tomatoes

6 organic eggs

½ teaspoon salt

½ teaspoon pepper

1 tablespoon butter

½ cup heavy whipping cream

2 tablespoons cream cheese, chopped

½ cup shredded Cheddar cheese

24 silver-dollar pancakes

6 slices white bread or dried fruit bread, toasted and cut into 4 triangles each

12 breakfast sausage links and/or patties, cooked

18 slices bacon, cooked

1 (½-cup) ramekin warm maple syrup

1 (½-cup) ramekin honey

1 (½-cup) ramekin softened butter

24 cracker-cut slices white Cheddar cheese

1 wedge Gouda cheese

1 wedge soft Brie cheese

24 slices apple

1 (½-cup) ramekin softened cream cheese

16 ounces prosciutto, sliced

Cherry tomatoes and sliced beefsteak tomatoes

1 cup each blueberries, blackberries, and raspberries

3 bananas, cut into 1-inch slices

Fresh basil sprigs to taste

DIRECTIONS

Warm the walnuts and pistachios in a small skillet over medium-low heat. Drizzle with the honey and toss to coat. Sprinkle with salt to taste. Spread on parchment paper and separate with a fork. Let stand to cool completely. Spread the wheat toast with mashed avocado mixture and sprinkle with Dickey's Everything Bagel Rub. Top each with a slice of tomato and cut into 4 toast points. Preheat the oven to 350 degrees. Whisk the eggs, ½ teaspoon salt, and pepper in a bowl. Melt 1 tablespoon butter in a skillet over medium-high heat. Add the eggs and cook to medium consistency, stirring frequently. Add the heavy cream, cream cheese, and shredded Cheddar cheese. Pour into a small baking dish or divide among individual ramekins. Bake for 10 to 15 minutes or until set. Build the board with the honey-glazed nuts, avocado toast points, baked eggs, and remaining ingredients, arranging as desired.

 The phone eats first, so an Instagram-worthy brunch board is always a hit."

Chef Phil Butler's
CHEESY
SAUSAGE-STUFFED BREAD

Prep Time: 45 minutes   **Difficulty:** Medium   **Serves:** 6 to 8

INGREDIENTS

1 medium russet potato

¾ cup light olive oil

1 yellow onion, cut into ¼-inch slices

1 red bell pepper, seeded and cut into ¼-inch slices

1 green bell pepper, seeded and cut into ¼-inch slices

2 cloves garlic, thinly sliced

1 pound bulk Italian sweet sausage

1 large, long loaf soft Italian-style bread

8 slices provolone cheese, cut into halves

2 teaspoons garlic salt

DIRECTIONS

Wash the potato and cut lengthwise into halves. Cut each half crosswise into ¼-inch slices. Heat the olive oil to 325 degrees in a medium saucepan over medium-high heat. Add the potato, onion, and bell peppers. Fry for 5 minutes. Add the garlic. Cook until the onion and bell peppers are tender and have brown edges and the potatoes are brown and crisp.

Meanwhile, brown the Italian sausage in a large skillet, stirring to crumble; drain. Remove the potato mixture from the oil using a strainer and add to the sausage, reserving the frying oil. Toss the sausage and potato mixture to mix well. Remove from the heat.

Preheat the oven or a grill to 350 degrees. Cut the Italian bread crosswise into slits in 1-inch increments with a serrated knife, cutting three-fourths of the way through the loaf. Place the loaf on a large piece of foil. Place a slice of provolone cheese on one side of each slit and add about 3 tablespoons of the sausage mixture in each slit. Brush the surface lightly with 2 tablespoons of the reserved frying oil and sprinkle with the garlic salt. Wrap with the foil, leaving the top open slightly and twisting the ends. Bake or grill for 30 minutes. Pull slices apart and fold over to hold the sausage filling in place while eating. May chill the prepared sandwich for a few hours before baking if desired.

> 66 *Living in New Jersey, I was introduced to a few good sausage and burger joints. The fried hot dog 'Ripper' is interesting, but I fell in love with the simple but unique combination of a roasted sausage on a hoagie roll, topped with onions, peppers, and potatoes fried together in a large pan of olive oil. Sounds crazy, but it worked really well."*

BROWN SUGAR
WHISKEY WINGS

Prep Time: 1½ hours (plus 1 hour)   **Difficulty:** Easy   **Serves:** 4

INGREDIENTS

24 jumbo chicken wings, drums and flats

1 tablespoon kosher salt

2 tablespoons Louisiana-style hot sauce

1 cup Brown Sugar Whiskey Mop Sauce (recipe, page 92)

Ranch dressing, for serving

DIRECTIONS

Pat the chicken wings dry with a paper towel. Place the wings in a large bowl. Sprinkle with the salt and drizzle with the hot sauce. Toss to coat the wings evenly. Marinate in the refrigerator for 1 hour.

Heat the smoker to 190 to 200 degrees. Arrange the wings on the racks. Smoke for 40 to 50 minutes. Place the Brown Sugar Whiskey Mop Sauce in a heatproof bowl and heat in the smoker. Cook the wings until a meat thermometer inserted into the thickest portion registers 130 degrees. Remove to a platter.

Heat the smoker to 300 to 325 degrees. Toss the wings with a small amount of the mop sauce and arrange on the grill. Grill for 4 to 5 minutes. Baste the wings with mop sauce and turn the wings over. Baste again. Grill for 4 to 5 minutes and repeat basting, turning, and grilling two or three times or until a meat thermometer inserted into the thickest portion registers 165 degrees and the wings are slightly charred and sticky. Remove to a platter and let stand for 5 to 10 minutes. Serve with ranch dressing.

NOTE

Mop sauces are not just for smoking; they can be used for a glaze during medium-temperature grilling. However, be careful. Too high of a temperature may burn them and make them become bitter.

BARBECUE & BEYOND

It all started as a joke made over cocktails a decade ago. "Then we'll be ready for global barbecue domination!" Roland Dickey, Sr., said. Little did he know that turned on a lightbulb for Roland Dickey, Jr., that would guide Dickey, Jr., to expand the Dickey Family portfolio of businesses to include retail products, manufacturers, real estate, metal fabrication, and distribution companies. With Dickey, Jr., at the helm, the family legacy continues to grow exponentially, with the first three international locations opened in the Middle East in 2018. The world's largest barbecue franchise opened its fourth and fifth international locations in Tokyo and Singapore in 2021, and international expansion partners built in Singapore, Brazil, and Australia.

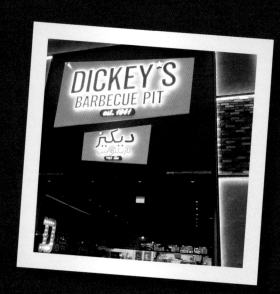

Early on, Roland, Jr., knew that if you can dream it, you can build it. He focused on expanding the Dickey Family portfolio to better support the restaurants and launched stainless steel and custom millwork, as well as full restaurant equipment packages. With an experienced team of engineers and craftsmen readily available to deliver quality goods, Roland, Jr., launched Stanford Sonoma. Longtime Dickey's Vice President Trinity Hall spent more than a decade using her experience to lead growth at Dickey's and was tapped to become the President for Stanford Sonoma Corporation. As a woman-owned company, she leads the charge for all product innovation and oversees the design and construction of all Stanford Sonoma projects internationally. "Trinity's work ethic and commitment are outstanding." Roland, Jr., says, "She and I share the same kind of work crazy, and we all trust and respect her immensely."

Chef Phil, Nick, Roland, Jr., Randy, Shayla, and Laura Rea

Another way to serve Dickey's guests was to launch Barbecue at Home in 2019. Spearheaded by Shayla Partusch, Barbecue at Home was born out of the desire to give folks the same quality Dickey's offers in their restaurants but with the convenience of cooking at home. Barbecue lovers can purchase one-of-a-kind barbecue products, hand-cut meats, and more online, and it will be delivered to their doorstep. "Shayla really understood the vision and possibilities of our retail program and barbecueathome.com," says Roland, Jr. "She is a great negotiator, is a fierce project manager, and has helped us build this side of the business for our guests from the ground up."

HONEY SERRANO
CHICKEN WINGS

Prep Time: 70 to 85 minutes (plus 1 hour)   **Difficulty:** Easy   **Serves:** 4

INGREDIENTS

24 jumbo chicken wings, drums and flats

2 teaspoons kosher salt

1 tablespoon vodka

2 serrano peppers, thinly sliced

2 tablespoons honey

1 tablespoon Dickey's Everything Bagel Rub

¼ cup chopped fresh cilantro

DIRECTIONS

Pat the chicken wings dry with a paper towel and place the wings in a large bowl. Sprinkle with the salt and drizzle with the vodka. Toss to coat the wings evenly. Marinate in the refrigerator for 1 hour.

Heat the smoker to 225 degrees. Arrange the wings on the racks. Smoke for 50 to 60 minutes. Cook the wings until a meat thermometer inserted into the thickest portion registers 165 degrees. Arrange on a wire rack in a baking sheet. Let stand for 10 to 15 minutes.

Preheat a convection oven or tabletop air fryer to 375 degrees. Cook the wings for 10 minutes or until crisp. Arrange the serrano peppers in a large bowl. Place the hot wings on top of the peppers, allowing the heat of the wings to release the flavor and spice in the peppers. Drizzle the hot wings with the honey and sprinkle with the Dickey's Everything Bagel Rub, tossing constantly. Remove the wings and peppers to a plate and sprinkle with the cilantro. Serve immediately.

NOTE

Everyone enjoys crispy skin on chicken wings, but smoking does not yield that expected crunch. Using a tabletop air fryer or convection oven after smoking will crisp the skins.

DR PEPPER® BACON-WRAPPED CHICKEN LOLLIPOPS

Prep Time: 45 minutes (plus ½ to 6 hours)   **Difficulty:** Medium   **Serves:** 6 to 8

INGREDIENTS

8 chicken drumsticks

2 tablespoons Chili Pork Rub (recipe, page 78), or any sweet barbecue rub

8 slices bacon

1 cup Dr Pepper Barbecue Sauce (recipe, page 90)

Dr Pepper Barbecue Sauce, for serving

DIRECTIONS

Cut the skin and meat 1½ inches from the knuckles of the drumsticks using a sharp boning knife, cutting down to the bone around the entire leg. Pull the meat and knuckle from the bone and discard; this creates the lollipop.

Season the drumsticks evenly with the Chili Pork Rub. Wrap a slice of bacon around the meat of each drumstick, securing with a wooden pick. Wrap the exposed bone with foil and arrange the drumsticks on a plate. Marinate in the refrigerator for 30 minutes or up to 6 hours.

Heat a grill or pellet-style smoker to 225 degrees, preparing the grill for indirect heat. Arrange the lollipops on the grill or on the top rack of the smoker. Grill for 15 to 20 minutes or until the bacon is rendered and a meat thermometer inserted into the thickest portion of the chicken registers 125 to 130 degrees. May grill using a chicken leg hanging rack with a pan below.

Heat 1 cup Dr Pepper Barbecue Sauce in a small saucepan over medium heat. Dip each lollipop into the sauce, covering the entire meaty area and returning to the grill. Grill until a meat thermometer inserted into the thickest portion registers 175 to 185 degrees; do not overcook. Remove to a plate and let stand for 10 minutes. Serve with additional Dr Pepper Barbecue Sauce.

NOTE

By combining the classic flavors and textures of chicken, bacon, and Dr Pepper, these appetizers will become a family favorite after just one try.

Pit Master Jeremy Dykes'
TEXAS-STYLE
CHICKEN DIP

PIT MASTER APPROVED

Prep Time: 3½ to 4½ beers (or 1 hour)   **Difficulty:** Easy   **Serves:** 8 to 10

INGREDIENTS

2 pounds smoked chicken

¾ cup Dickey's Original Barbecue Sauce

⅓ cup Buffalo-style wing sauce

1 tablespoon brown sugar

1 teaspoon Dickey's Rib Rub

1 tablespoon Dickey's Beef Brisket Rub

8 ounces cream cheese, softened

2 cups shredded sharp Cheddar cheese

¼ cup sliced green onions, for garnish

Chips or crackers, for serving

DIRECTIONS

Preheat a grill, pit, or oven to 325 degrees. Shred the chicken in a large bowl. Combine the Dickey's Original Barbecue Sauce, wing sauce, and brown sugar in a bowl and whisk until smooth. Combine 1 cup of the sauce, Dickey's Rib Rub, and Dickey's Beef Brisket Rub in a small bowl and mix well. Add to the chicken and mix gently with a rubber spatula until the chicken is evenly coated. Add the cream cheese and 1¾ cups of the Cheddar cheese and mix well. Spread evenly in a 9x13-inch foil pan. Sprinkle evenly with the remaining ¼ cup Cheddar cheese and drizzle with the remaining sauce. Smoke for 30 to 45 minutes or bake for 20 to 30 minutes or until hot and bubbly. Garnish with the green onions and serve with chips or crackers. Pairs well with an All Day IPA or Sweetwater 420.

NOTE

The flavor profile of this dish goes great with a good IPA. Founder All Day IPA or Sweetwater 420 are my favorites.

" *My family enjoys this easy Texas twist on chicken dip and really kicks up the flavor for game day!*"

Michelle Matthews'
FIVE-MINUTE
BUFFALO CHICKEN DIP

Prep Time: 5 minutes   **Difficulty:** Easy   **Serves:** 5 to 8

INGREDIENTS

1 pound Dickey's Marinated Chicken Breasts, chopped

8 ounces light or regular cream cheese

1 pint hot or mild Dickey's Buffalo Sauce

1 package scoopable corn chips, tortilla chips, and/or celery sticks, for serving

DIRECTIONS

Place the Dickey's Marinated Chicken Breasts in a microwave-safe bowl. Microwave for 1 minute. Add the cream cheese. Microwave for 1 minute. Add half of the Dickey's Buffalo Sauce and stir until smooth. Microwave for 1 minute or until heated through. Stir in the desired amount of the remaining Dickey's Buffalo Sauce. Serve with chips and/or celery.

NOTE

Whether it's a perfectly planned-out party or last-minute neighborhood get-together, or if you forgot you were nominated to provide a potluck side at work, this Buffalo Chicken Dip recipe is a crowd-pleaser you can make in FIVE minutes!

 Caution: You will likely get a lot of compliments, so be sure to have your backstory straight on how many hours it took you to slow-smoke your own chicken, etc., etc."

FRIED
GREEN TOMATOES

Prep Time: 15 minutes   **Difficulty:** Medium   **Serves:** 4

INGREDIENTS

2 firm green tomatoes

¼ cup buttermilk

½ cup yellow cornmeal

½ cup all-purpose flour

1 teaspoon garlic salt

½ teaspoon black pepper

Vegetable oil, for frying

Dickey's Foo Foo Finishing Blend to taste

DIRECTIONS

Cut the stems from the tomatoes and discard. Cut the tomatoes crosswise into ½-inch slices. Pat the slices dry with paper towels.

Pour the buttermilk into a shallow bowl. Combine the cornmeal, flour, garlic salt, and pepper in a second shallow bowl and mix well. Dip the tomato slices into the buttermilk and coat completely with the cornmeal mixture.

Heat 1½ inches of vegetable oil to 375 degrees in a medium saucepan; oil will be shimmery. Fry 2 or 3 tomato slices at a time for 2 minutes. Turn the slices over using a slotted spoon. Fry for 1½ to 2 minutes or until golden brown. Remove to paper towels to drain. Sprinkle with Dickey's Foo Foo Finishing Blend.

NOTE

Be sure to use firm green tomatoes. If they are even a slight bit yellow, they are too soft and the breading will not stay on during frying.

Roland Dickey, Jr.'s
TACO DINNER
BOARD

Prep Time: 20 to 30 minutes **Difficulty:** Easy **Serves:** 6

INGREDIENTS

1 cup shredded lettuce

½ cup diced tomatoes

½ onion, chopped

1 pound ground turkey or other meat, cooked and seasoned

½ cup shredded Cheddar cheese

½ cup corn salsa

Sour cream to taste

Guacamole to taste

Sliced olives to taste

Chopped fresh cilantro to taste

Taco sauce to taste

Tortilla chips

6 taco shells

DIRECTIONS Season a large board for food or line with parchment paper. Build the board with a bowl of the lettuce and tomatoes in the center and small bowls of the remaining ingredients around the center bowl. Arrange the taco shells around the edges.

66 *I like to make this recipe on Taco Tuesdays.*"

Tanya Pollock's
PICKLED
SHRIMP

HOME OFFICE
GREATS

Prep Time: 10 minutes (plus 24 hours) **Difficulty:** Easy **Serves:** 8 to 10

INGREDIENTS

1 Vidalia or other sweet onion, thinly sliced

1 lemon, thinly sliced

¾ cup apple cider vinegar

½ cup canola oil

¼ cup capers with liquid

¾ teaspoon celery seeds

½ teaspoon sugar

½ teaspoon salt

Tabasco sauce to taste

1½ pounds 41/50 count shrimp, peeled and cooked

Saltine crackers, for serving

DIRECTIONS

Combine the onion, lemon, vinegar, canola oil, capers, celery seeds, sugar, salt, and Tabasco sauce in a large bowl and mix well. Add the shrimp and toss to mix. Spoon into a large glass jar, pressing to ensure all ingredients are submersed; cover tightly. May leave in mixing bowl and cover.

Chill for 24 hours or longer, stirring occasionally. Serve chilled with saltine crackers. May be stored in the refrigerator for about 1 week.

❝ I also like to add some pickled cut okra and dried red chili pods to the jar to add flavor and dress up the look.❞

Shayla Partusch's
POBLANO
QUESO

Prep Time: 30 minutes   **Difficulty:** Medium   **Serves:** 6 to 10

INGREDIENTS

4 poblano peppers

3 tablespoons butter

1 tablespoon olive oil

½ yellow onion, diced

3 cloves garlic, minced

4 tablespoons all-purpose flour

½ teaspoon ground cumin

2 cups whole milk

6 ounces cream cheese, cut into cubes

8 ounces sharp white Cheddar cheese, shredded

3 tablespoons chopped cilantro

½ teaspoon salt

¼ teaspoon freshly ground black pepper

DIRECTIONS

Preheat a grill or oven to 275 to 300 degrees. Arrange the poblano peppers on a wire rack in a grill or firepit. Char the peppers with a propane torch, turning to char evenly. Grill or bake for 5 minutes or until tender. Remove from the heat. Scrape the skins off the peppers using the edge of a knife; do not cut or rinse the peppers. Stem and seed the peppers. Cut into ¼-inch pieces.

Heat the grill to 350 to 375 degrees. Melt the butter in a Dutch oven on the grill or stovetop. Add the olive oil. Cook the onion and garlic in the butter mixture until tender, stirring frequently. Stir in the peppers. Cook, covered, for 2 to 3 minutes. Sprinkle with the flour and cumin and stir until well mixed. Cook, covered, for 2 to 3 minutes. Whisk in the milk until smooth. Bring just to a simmer and cook until thickened, stirring constantly. Add the cream cheese and Cheddar cheese. Cook until the mixture is smooth, stirring constantly with a spoon. Season with the cilantro, salt, and pepper. Serve immediately.

NOTE

You can make this with Hatch peppers, but fresh poblanos are available all year long, and when roasted have a deep green pepper flavor with medium spice notes.

This queso is mild and absolutely delicious. Whether we are grilling in the backyard or hosting game night with friends and family, this Poblano Queso is scoopable and gooey, making it undeniable for any cheese lover out there."

SMOKED ONION DIP

Prep Time: 2 hours (plus 1 hour)   **Difficulty:** Easy   **Serves:** 8 to 10

INGREDIENTS

4 sweet onions, cut into quarters

2 cups mayonnaise

2 cups sour cream

½ cup half-and-half

2 tablespoons Worcestershire sauce

1 tablespoon sugar

1 teaspoon granulated garlic

½ teaspoon kosher salt

½ teaspoon freshly ground black pepper

¼ cup finely chopped scallions, divided

DIRECTIONS

Preheat a pit to 275 to 300 degrees. Arrange the sweet onions on the rack of the pit. Smoke for 1½ hours or until tender and dark brown. Remove to a plate. Let stand to cool completely. Place the onions in a food processor and pulse until finely chopped.

Combine the mayonnaise, sour cream, half-and-half, Worcestershire sauce, sugar, granulated garlic, salt, and pepper in a large bowl and stir to mix. Add the sweet onions and half of the scallions and mix well. Spoon into a serving bowl and sprinkle with the remaining scallions. Chill for 1 hour before serving.

NOTE

Although this recipe has many of the same ingredients found in countless other dips (i.e., mayonnaise, sour cream, half-and-half, Worcestershire sauce), smoking the onion with hickory adds a rich, peppery flavor you won't find in store-bought dips. You may end up bypassing the chips and just eating it with a spoon.

SMOKY
DEVILED EGGS

Prep Time: 30 minutes   **Difficulty:** Easy   **Serves:** 6

INGREDIENTS

12 large eggs

6 tablespoons mayonnaise

2 teaspoons Dijon mustard

2 teaspoons apple
cider vinegar

1 teaspoon Tabasco sauce

Salt and pepper to taste

1 teaspoon paprika

Brisket burnt ends, smoked
ham, blackened shrimp,
or cedar-plank salmon,
for topping

DIRECTIONS

Place the eggs in a single layer in a large saucepan. Add enough water to cover the eggs by 1½ inches. Bring to a boil over high heat. Cover and reduce the heat to low. Cook for 1 minute. Remove from the heat. Let stand, covered, for 12 minutes. Remove the eggs to an ice bath to stop the cooking process. Peel the eggs under cool running water and pat dry with paper towels. Cut the eggs lengthwise into halves, placing the yolks in a bowl and the egg whites on an egg plate.

Mash the egg yolks with a fork until finely crumbled. Add the mayonnaise, mustard, vinegar, Tabasco sauce, salt, and pepper and mix well. Spoon the mixture into a piping bag. Fill each egg half evenly with the deviled filling. Sprinkle with the paprika and add desired toppings.

NOTE

There are tons of recipes for deviled eggs with unique fillings. Have some fun with this and top your deviled eggs with whatever you want to impress your guests!

Chef Phil Butler's
SMOKED TOMATO
BASIL SOUP

Prep Time: 2 hours (plus 3 to 4 hours)   **Difficulty:** Medium   **Serves:** 6 to 8

INGREDIENTS

4 pounds ripe
Roma tomatoes

¼ cup extra-virgin olive oil

1 yellow onion,
finely chopped

4 cloves garlic, minced

4 cups chicken stock

¼ cup sherry vinegar

2 cups heavy cream

¼ cup chopped fresh
basil leaves

2 teaspoons sea salt

¾ teaspoon freshly ground
black pepper

8 ounces smoked
Polish kielbasa, cut into
½-inch cubes

Chopped fresh basil,
for garnish

Crusty French bread,
for serving

DIRECTIONS

Soak 2 cups oak chips in water for 3 to 4 hours. Heat charcoal in a kettle grill or barrel smoker until evenly heated and covered with white ash. Move the charcoal to one side of the grill or smoker.

Cut the stems from the tomatoes. Cut the tomatoes lengthwise into halves. Arrange cut sides down on a wire rack and place in the grill or smoker. Place the prepared wood chips over the charcoal and close the lid. Smoke for 1½ hours.

Heat the olive oil in a large saucepan over medium heat. Add the onion and garlic and cook for 1 to 2 minutes or until tender but not brown. Add the tomatoes, chicken stock, and vinegar. Simmer for 30 minutes. Add the cream, ¼ cup basil, sea salt, and pepper. Bring to a boil and cook for 5 minutes. Blend the tomato mixture carefully using an immersion blender until smooth or cool slightly and process in batches in a blender.

Brown the kielbasa on all sides in a sauté pan and stir into the soup. Ladle the soup into soup bowls and garnish with basil. Serve with French bread.

66 *One of the first smoked items I ever did in a restaurant at the age of fourteen was smoked tomatoes for this soup. The rich smoke and heavy cream balance against the sherry vinegar and fresh basil.*"

SALADS

SMOKED BRISKET
WEDGE SALAD

Prep Time: 35 minutes   **Difficulty:** Medium   **Serves:** 4

INGREDIENTS

12 ounces leftover smoked brisket point (deckle), diced

2 teaspoons Dickey's Rib Rub or Chili Pork Rub (recipe, page 78)

¾ cup Dickey's Original Barbecue Sauce, divided

2 romaine hearts

½ cup crumbled blue cheese dressing

1 cup red and yellow grape tomato halves

½ cup chopped crisp bacon, about ¼-inch pieces

4 tablespoons sliced chives, about ¼-inch pieces

½ teaspoon freshly ground black pepper

DIRECTIONS

Preheat a smoker or oven to 275 degrees. Spread the brisket on a foil-lined baking sheet. Sprinkle with the Dickey's Rib Rub and drizzle with ½ cup of the Dickey's Original Barbecue Sauce. Toss gently with a rubber spatula until the brisket is evenly coated. Smoke or bake for 20 to 25 minutes or until the brisket is heated through, stirring every 10 minutes with the spatula to ensure even glazing. Let stand to rest for 10 minutes.

Cut the romaine hearts lengthwise into halves. Cut the stem in a V shape and discard the stem. Cut the halves lengthwise into halves. Arrange the romaine leaves on a large board or platter, alternating leafy and stem ends. Drizzle with the blue cheese dressing and sprinkle with the tomatoes and bacon.

Toss the brisket with the remaining ¼ cup Dickey's Original Barbecue Sauce. Arrange the brisket evenly over the salad, including any remaining sauce. Sprinkle with the chives and pepper. Serve with a large spatula for easy portioning.

NOTE

Smoked brisket is a versatile leftover, and this wedge is an ideal pairing. When reheating in this fashion, use the point or deckle because it has marbled fat and moisture in contrast to the lean, flat portion of the brisket. The process is similar to making brisket burnt ends.

Ed Herman's
PULLED CHICKEN
SALAD

Prep Time: 15 to 20 minutes **Difficulty:** Easy **Serves:** 6 to 8

INGREDIENTS

¾ cup mayonnaise

¼ cup sour cream or plain Greek yogurt

2 tablespoons apple cider vinegar

Juice of ½ lemon

½ teaspoon kosher salt

½ teaspoon freshly ground black pepper

4 cups crosscut shredded cooked chicken

½ cup finely chopped sweet onion

½ cup finely chopped celery

DIRECTIONS

Combine the mayonnaise, sour cream, vinegar, lemon juice, salt, and pepper in a large bowl and mix with a rubber spatula. Add the chicken, onion, and celery and mix well. Serve immediately or chill in an airtight container until serving time.

 I make this salad with any type of leftover chicken: grilled chicken breasts, rotisserie chicken, or even fried chicken (minus the breading!). Pulled Chicken Salad on Texas toast is simple and satisfying. Finely chop the chicken and then add chopped pickled jalapeños and a few dashes of hot sauce for a flavorful dip with crackers. If your chicken is a little dry, you can add ¼ cup of chicken stock to revive it!"

Mrs. Dickey's
EAST TEXAS
ITALIAN SALAD

Prep Time: 15 minutes **Difficulty:** Easy **Serves:** 8

INGREDIENTS

4 cups mixed baby greens

4 cups chopped romaine hearts, about
1- to 1½-inch pieces

1½ cups drained Italian olive salad

2 medium Creole or other tomatoes,
cut into wedges

8 cloves garlic, cut into paper-thin slices

Italian Dressing (recipe, page 99)

16 anchovies in oil, drained

8 asparagus spears, steamed and chilled

8 cooked preboiled 16/20 shrimp

¼ cup freshly grated Romano cheese

DIRECTIONS

Combine the baby greens, romaine, olive salad, tomatoes, garlic, and Italian Dressing in a
large bowl and toss with salad tongs.

Divide the salad evenly among 8 salad plates, distributing the olive salad and tomatoes
evenly. Arrange 2 anchovies in an X pattern on top of each salad. Add 1 asparagus spear
and 1 shrimp. Sprinkle with the Romano cheese and serve immediately.

NOTE

*It's a little-known fact that Mr. Dickey makes this salad for Mrs. Dickey (also known as Big
Mama) on a regular basis.*

SHE SAVED MY LIFE, SO I'M OBLIGATED TO COOK FOR HER

I never eat meat by myself. Not that I don't love meat. I just have a phobia that I might choke and not have anybody there to perform the Heimlich maneuver. I always kid around that I'm not sure if Big Mama would do the Heimlich for me, but that's a joke. One time I was eating steak in a restaurant in Dallas, and I actually did choke. I couldn't swallow or breath and was pretty sure that bite of rib eye was my last. I briefly regretted that it wasn't a bite of filet mignon because that seemed like a classier way to go out, but there I was—panicked. Then, around the table came Maurine, and she gave me the Heimlich maneuver and saved my life. Now, I know a lot of people wouldn't have bet that way, but she saved my life and got a chance to hit me in public, too. Win-win. It's probably fifty-fifty she'd still do that today.

So, I am officially obligated to cook for her for the rest of my life. When I do cook for her, I might do something elaborate, because I want to keep her happy. I often make fish for her, or grilled octopus. When I make food for myself, I do the simplest recipes possible—they've got to be cheap, fast and, of course, delicious. That's why I consider myself a short-order, gourmet cook. There are lots of ways to end up with a great dish, but somehow it tastes better to me if you've found a quick work-around. So, I recommend using shortcut ingredients. For example, don't mince garlic; buy it minced. Use Campbell's® soup bases. Add spices, especially pepper, and don't worry about complicated ingredients. That's my philosophy on cooking.

Mr. and Mrs. Dickey

GRILLED APPLE & ENDIVE SALAD

Prep Time: 40 minutes   **Difficulty:** Medium   **Serves:** 6 to 8

INGREDIENTS

3 Granny Smith apples

3 heads endive

½ cup Maytag or other blue cheese, crumbled

2 tablespoons chopped fresh parsley

½ cup honey-roasted pecans or walnuts

½ cup Simple Citrus Vinaigrette (recipe, page 99)

½ teaspoon freshly ground black pepper

DIRECTIONS

Preheat a grill to 400 degrees, using oak charcoal or pellets.

Cut the apples into halves and core each half. Cut the apples lengthwise into ¼-inch slices. Arrange on the grill rack and grill one side for 2 minutes. Remove to a plate and chill in the refrigerator.

Cut the endive lengthwise into halves, cut the stem in a V shape, and discard the stem. Cut the endive lengthwise into ⅛-inch strips.

Combine the cooled apples, endive, blue cheese, parsley, pecans, Simple Citrus Vinaigrette, and pepper in a large bowl and toss gently to mix; do not overmix. Serve immediately.

NOTE

The sweet grilled apple and citrus vinaigrette balance the flavor of the slightly bitter endive. Due to the flavor and salt content, Maytag blue cheese is recommended, but any blue cheese will work well.

66 *Roasted beets from the grill are amazing, but once the packaged cooked beets hit the grocery store shelves, they are my go-to! Since they are cooked, I can take advantage of tossing them in a marinade with herbs and placing them right on the grill to char the pieces! No dressing is needed; the pickled red onions, avocado, and goat cheese add all the flavor needed. Do not toss this salad; the beets stain everything, and you want to keep the flavors and colors separate."*

Jamie Henretta's
GRILLED BEET &
GOAT CHEESE SALAD

Prep Time: 20 to 30 minutes   **Difficulty:** Easy   **Serves:** 4 to 6

INGREDIENTS

1 (8.8-ounce) package cooked whole beets

¼ cup Red Meat Oil Marinade (recipe, page 83)

1 ripe avocado

1 cup torn arugula

¼ cup crumbled goat cheese

¼ cup Sweet Chili Pickled Red Onions (recipe, page 84)

Freshly ground black pepper to taste

DIRECTIONS

Preheat a grill to 400 degrees, using mesquite charcoal. Cut the beets into ¾- to 1-inch pieces. Combine the beets and Red Meat Oil Marinade in a bowl and toss to coat. Marinate for 10 to 15 minutes. Arrange the beets on a wire rack and place the rack on the grill grate. Smoke, covered, for 3 to 4 minutes. Roll the beets over, using tongs. Grill, covered, for 3 to 4 minutes. Remove to a plate. Let stand to cool for 10 to 15 minutes.

Cut the avocado into halves and remove the peeling and seed using a spoon. Cut into ½-inch pieces.

Layer the arugula, beets, and avocado on a serving plate. Sprinkle with the goat cheese and Sweet Chili Pickled Red Onions. Season with pepper and serve.

Renee Roozen's
GRILLED CITRUS &
WATERMELON SALAD

Prep Time: 45 minutes   **Difficulty:** Medium   **Serves:** 8 to 10

INGREDIENTS

2 pounds seedless watermelon

3 navel oranges

2 blood oranges

1 grapefruit

½ red onion, finely diced

5 sprigs of fresh mint, chopped

¾ cup Simple Citrus Vinaigrette (recipe, page 99)

Salt and pepper to taste (optional)

DIRECTIONS

Preheat a grill to 350 to 400 degrees, using oak charcoal. Peel the watermelon and cut into 1-inch pieces, placing in a large bowl. Cut off and discard the ends of the navel oranges, blood oranges, and grapefruit, cutting through the pith. Cut the oranges and grapefruit crosswise into 1-inch slices. Arrange the slices on the grill grate and grill for 3 minutes or until grill marks form. Turn the slices over and grill for 3 to 4 minutes. Remove to a large plate and chill in the refrigerator.

Cut the peeling on one side of each orange and grapefruit slice and pull the peeling off. Add the oranges and grapefruit to the watermelon and toss with a rubber spatula. Add the onion, mint, Simple Citrus Vinaigrette, salt, and pepper and toss to mix. Let stand for 15 minutes before serving.

NOTE

Watermelon's peak season is May through September. When I make this recipe, I grill the citrus to reduce some of the acidity. The sweetness of the fresh watermelon and grilled citrus blend perfectly with lemon dressing. You can add feta cheese to this salad, but I like to keep it simple. Also, as a side note, this mixture—minus the vinaigrette and red onion—is great muddled into margaritas!

"Woo-hoo! I love to make this recipe in the summertime! The sweetness of the fresh watermelon and grilled citrus are balanced with a lemon dressing, making it the perfect light combination."

RAMEN NOODLE
BROCCOLI SALAD

Prep Time: 15 to 20 minutes **Difficulty:** Easy **Serves:** 7 to 8

INGREDIENTS

1 pound bacon

1 cup Simple Citrus Vinaigrette (recipe, page 99)

2 packages chicken-flavor ramen noodles
with flavor packet

1 head broccoli, cut into small pieces

1 cup shredded carrots

½ red onion, finely diced

½ cup dried cranberries

1 cup honey-roasted pecans, chopped

DIRECTIONS

Cut the bacon crosswise into 1-inch pieces and place in a medium saucepan. Cook over medium heat until brown and crisp. Remove to paper towels to drain. Let stand to cool.

Combine the Simple Citrus Vinaigrette and 1 flavor packet from the ramen noodles in a large bowl and whisk until smooth. Add the broccoli, carrots, onion, dried cranberries, pecans, and bacon and mix well.

Crush the ramen noodles by hand into small pieces. Add to the salad and toss to mix. Let stand for 15 to 20 minutes before serving.

GRILLED CORN & OKRA
SALAD

Prep Time: 1 hour (plus 30 minutes)   **Difficulty:** Medium   **Serves:** 4 to 6

INGREDIENTS

3 tablespoons olive oil

½ teaspoon ground cumin

½ teaspoon ground black pepper

½ teaspoon granulated garlic

3 ears yellow corn, husks and silks removed

1 poblano pepper

12 medium okra, stemmed

1 cup grape tomato halves

1 cup seedless cucumber pieces, about ½ inch

½ red onion, cut into halves and sliced

¼ cup chopped fresh cilantro

Juice of 4 limes

1 teaspoon kosher salt

1 teaspoon sugar

DIRECTIONS

Preheat a grill to 400 to 450 degrees, using mesquite charcoal or pellets. Combine the olive oil, cumin, black pepper, and granulated garlic in a large bowl and mix well. Add the corn, poblano pepper, and okra and toss and brush to coat evenly. Arrange the corn on the grill. Grill for 5 minutes or until charred. Rotate a quarter turn and repeat the procedure until all 4 sides are charred. Remove to a tray to cool. Place the poblano pepper on the grill. Grill for 5 minutes or until charred. Rotate a third turn and repeat the procedure until all 3 sides are charred. Remove to the tray with the corn. Arrange the okra on the grill, reserving the olive oil mixture. Grill for 2 minutes or until charred. Rotate a quarter turn and repeat the procedure until all 4 sides are charred. Remove to the tray with the corn. Let the vegetables stand to cool for 20 minutes.

Cut the corn from the cobs using a sharp knife. Cut the poblano pepper into halves, remove the stem and seeds, and cut into ¼-inch pieces. Cut the okra crosswise into ½-inch pieces. Add the corn, poblano pepper, and okra to the reserved olive oil mixture and toss to coat. Add the tomatoes, cucumbers, onion, cilantro, lime juice, salt, and sugar and toss to mix. Let stand to marinate for 30 minutes before serving.

LOOK, MA, I'M ON TV!

Through the years, Dickey's has had a few ambassadors represent the brand—most notably, Roland Dickey, Sr. Mr. Dickey, who became locally famous just for being himself, starred in his own television commercials for years. He also represented Dickey's on news channels by doing cooking segments and interviews. *Live with Regis and Kelly* had Mr. Dickey and Roland, Jr., as guests for a barbecue segment, where they fired up a grill just outside the studio on the busy streets of New York. These days, Mr. Dickey still does appearances on television, and he also is joined by his daughter-in-law Laura Rea Dickey and Dickey's corporate chef, Phil Butler. Laura also has taken up the torch as spokesperson, appearing regularly on national news

segments as an industry expert and international business owner.

"I wanted to be a lawyer, but I was twenty when my dad passed, and I had to take over the one barbecue stand to take care of my mom. We had $5,000 in life insurance—enough for the funeral—with $1,500 left to keep ordering food for the restaurant. That was it. Man, I was going to work right then. We only had a few recipes from him, so I had to get on that, too. I found that the more I talked to folks and was able to connect with them, the more business grew. One day, I was able to tell my mom we'd started to make it: 'Look, Ma, I'm on TV!'" says Roland, Sr.

Roland giving a cooking demonstration with host Rebecca Miller of NBC 5 television

Live with Regis and Kelly featuring Dickey's Barbecue

Trinity Hall's
ROASTED CORN
ELOTE SALAD

Prep Time: 2 hours   **Difficulty:** Easy   **Serves:** 4 to 6

INGREDIENTS

4 ears yellow corn in husks

2 tablespoons mayonnaise

1 tablespoon sour cream

¼ teaspoon garlic powder

Juice of ½ lime

½ teaspoon kosher salt

¼ cup finely chopped red onion

¼ cup crumbled cotija cheese

½ cup chopped fresh cilantro

Dickey's Rib Rub or cayenne pepper to taste

DIRECTIONS

Preheat the oven to 450 degrees, moving the oven rack to the middle position. Arrange the corn on a baking sheet. Bake for 30 minutes or until husks are brown and dry. Let stand to cool for 1½ hours.

Combine the mayonnaise, sour cream, garlic powder, lime juice, and salt in a bowl and mix with a rubber spatula. Stir in the onion, cotija cheese, and cilantro.

Peel and silk the corn. Cut the corn from the cobs using a sharp knife and separate the kernels if needed. Add the corn to the mayonnaise mixture and mix with the rubber spatula. Spoon into a serving bowl and sprinkle with Dickey's Rib Rub.

66 *This recipe is creamy, flavorful delicious, and perfect for summer cookouts, especially when sweet corn is in season through the hotter months."*

GREEN BEAN
SALAD

Prep Time: 15 minutes   **Difficulty:** Easy   **Serves:** 6 to 8

INGREDIENTS

1 gallon water

2 tablespoons kosher salt

1½ pounds fresh green beans, trimmed

2 tablespoons soy sauce

1 tablespoon sugar

1 tablespoon red wine vinegar

4 sweet peppers, seeded and cut crosswise into ¼-inch pieces

1 tablespoon Dickey's Everything Bagel Rub

DIRECTIONS

Combine the water and salt in a large pot. Bring to a boil over high heat. Add the green beans and cook for 4 minutes or until crisp-tender; drain. Plunge into a bowl of ice water.

Combine the soy sauce, sugar and vinegar in a small bowl and mix with a fork until the sugar is dissolved. Drain the cooled green beans. Combine the green beans, sweet peppers, and soy sauce mixture in a large bowl and toss to mix. Sprinkle with the Dickey's Everything Bagel Rub. Spoon into a serving bowl.

NOTE

The essential ingredient for this recipe is Dickey's Everything Bagel Rub, which makes this Green Bean Salad uniquely simple.

Mr. Dickey's
CAPRESE
SALAD

Prep Time: 5 minutes   **Difficulty:** Easy   **Serves:** 1 to 2

INGREDIENTS

2 beefsteak tomatoes, chopped

½ sweet onion, chopped

1 (4- to 5-ounce) ball fresh mozzarella cheese, chopped

Vinaigrette of choice

DIRECTIONS   Combine the tomatoes, onion, and mozzarella cheese on a plate. Drizzle the vinaigrette over the top and serve.

66 *Here's how I make this recipe. Use one ball of fresh mozzarella cheese, two whole tomatoes, half of a sweet onion, and vinaigrette dressing. That's the whole thing. Chop up the cheese, tomatoes, and onion, toss together, and then add the vinaigrette. Now, this salad is big enough as an appetizer for two people. I'll probably make it tonight. If it's just you, it's a meal; that's it. There ain't nothing else coming. Ain't no steak or nothing! Now on the tomatoes: Big Mama wants me to get heirlooms, not the hothouse. I mean, I think most of the tomatoes in America are hothouse. In the wintertime, they all are, but you know, they're from Mexico. If I use heirloom tomatoes, they might be from America, but those are so soft and mushy, especially if you hold them for a day or two at home. Big Mama thinks she's eating heirloom tomatoes all the time. Well, they're not; they're hothouse tomatoes."*

CUCUMBER TOMATO SALAD

Prep Time: 5 to 6 minutes   **Difficulty:** Easy   **Serves:** 6 to 8

INGREDIENTS
3 cucumbers

3 beefsteak tomatoes

½ red onion, finely chopped

3 tablespoons chopped fresh parsley

¾ cup Simple Citrus Vinaigrette (recipe, page 99)

DIRECTIONS
Peel the cucumbers and cut the ends off. Cut the cucumbers lengthwise into quarters and crosswise into 1-inch pieces. Core the tomatoes and cut into 1-inch cubes. Combine the cucumbers, tomatoes, onion, parsley, and Simple Citrus Vinaigrette in a large bowl. Let stand to marinate for 30 minutes before serving.

Laura Rea's grandmother, Nota McCulley, "Granny Mac"

Sandy Rea's
GRANNY MAC'S
CRANBERRY SALAD

Prep Time: 20 minutes (plus overnight)   **Difficulty:** Easy   **Serves:** 6 to 8

INGREDIENTS

12 ounces fresh cranberries

1 cup sugar

2 cups red seedless grape halves

4 ounces miniature marshmallows

8 ounces frozen whipped topping, thawed

¾ cup chopped pecans

DIRECTIONS

Process the cranberries in a food processor until finely chopped and spoon into a bowl. Add the sugar and mix well. Chill overnight to allow the sugar to sweeten the cranberries.

Drain the cranberries if needed. Combine the cranberries, grapes, marshmallows, whipped topping, and pecans in a bowl and mix with a rubber spatula; do not overmix. Spoon into a serving bowl. Chill until serving time.

Granny Mac's Cranberry Salad has been in my family on our holiday table my entire life. Cannot celebrate without it!"

RUBS,
SAUCES,
&PICKLES

CHILI PORK
RUB

Prep Time: 20 to 30 minutes   **Difficulty:** Medium   **Seasons:** 10 to 12 pounds

INGREDIENTS

2 dried ancho peppers

2 dried New Mexican chili peppers

1 dried chipotle pepper

¼ cup sweet Spanish paprika

2 tablespoons light brown sugar

1½ tablespoons sea salt

1 teaspoon celery salt

2 teaspoons ground cumin

2 teaspoons garlic powder

1 tablespoon fine-ground black pepper

1 tablespoon dry yellow mustard

DIRECTIONS

Preheat the oven to 350 degrees. Arrange the ancho peppers, New Mexican chili peppers, and chipotle pepper on a baking sheet. Bake for 2 minutes. Turn the peppers over using tongs. Bake for 2 minutes or until peppers are puffed. Let stand to cool for 15 to 20 minutes.

Remove the stems and shake out the seeds from each crisp pepper, using gloves to handle the peppers. Crush the peppers into a coffee grinder and pulse until powdery. Remove to a bowl. Add the paprika, brown sugar, sea salt, celery salt, cumin, garlic powder, black pepper, and dry mustard and whisk to mix well. May store in an airtight jar for up to 2 months.

NOTE

Buying chili powder works well, but toasting and grinding fresh chili peppers will make for a flavorful spice rub, marinade, or sauce. This rub works well on both grilled and slow-smoked barbecued meats.

RED MEAT
RUB

Prep Time: 6 to 8 minutes   **Difficulty:** Easy   **Seasons:** 6 to 8 pounds

INGREDIENTS

½ cup dried parsley

3 tablespoons granulated garlic

2 tablespoons ground coriander

2 tablespoons sea salt

2 tablespoons medium-ground black pepper

1 tablespoon granulated lemonade mix

1 tablespoon dry yellow mustard

¼ teaspoon cayenne pepper

DIRECTIONS

Combine the parsley, granulated garlic, coriander, salt, black pepper, lemonade mix, dry mustard, and cayenne pepper in a jar. Close the lid and shake to mix. May store in the airtight jar for up to 2 months.

NOTE

The addition of the lemonade mix may seem very odd, but the pop of citrus notes on beef reduces the need for more salt. The citrus flavor blended with garlic, black pepper, and yellow mustard adds a savory note to grilled red meats.

POULTRY
RUB

Prep Time: 5 to 10 minutes **Difficulty:** Easy **Seasons:** 10 to 12 pounds

---

INGREDIENTS

2 bay leaves, crumbled

3 tablespoons dried rosemary leaves

2 tablespoons dried thyme leaves

2 tablespoons dried Mexican oregano

2 tablespoons dried basil leaves

1 teaspoon dried sage leaves

1 tablespoon kosher salt

1 teaspoon ground coriander

1 teaspoon granulated onion

1 teaspoon celery salt

1 teaspoon fine-ground black pepper

DIRECTIONS

Place the bay leaves in a small bowl. Add the rosemary, thyme, oregano, basil, and sage and crush with the back of a spoon. Spoon into a jar. Add the salt, coriander, granulated onion, celery salt, and pepper. Cover and shake the jar to mix well. May store in the airtight jar for up to 2 months.

NOTE

Dry spice blends with herbs are always better when allowed to marinate for up to 3 hours prior to roasting or grilling poultry.

SEAFOOD & VEGETABLE RUB

Prep Time: 5 minutes   **Difficulty:** Easy   **Seasons:** 6 to 7 pounds

INGREDIENTS

½ cup garlic salt

¼ cup freshly ground black pepper

1 tablespoon white pepper

1 tablespoon dried marjoram

1 tablespoon smoked paprika

1 tablespoon dried basil

1 tablespoon dried lemon peel granules (optional)

2 teaspoons dried thyme

1 teaspoon dry mustard

DIRECTIONS

Combine the garlic salt, black pepper, white pepper, marjoram, paprika, basil, lemon peel granules, thyme, and dry mustard in a jar. Cover and shake to mix. May store in the airtight jar for up to 2 months.

THE SPRITZ

Prep Time: 6 to 8 minutes   **Difficulty:** Easy   **Seasons:** 6 to 8 pounds

INGREDIENTS

1 cup apple cider vinegar

3 tablespoons Worcestershire sauce

1 tablespoon bourbon

½ cup water

DIRECTIONS

Combine the vinegar, Worcestershire sauce, bourbon, and water in a spray bottle and shake to mix well.

RED CHILI
RUB

Prep Time: 6 to 8 minutes (plus 12 hours)   **Difficulty:** Easy   **Seasons:** 12 to 18 pounds

INGREDIENTS

1 (10-ounce) can mild or hot enchilada sauce

3 tablespoons chili powder

2 tablespoons paprika

2 tablespoons ground cumin

1 tablespoon ground coriander

1 tablespoon ground Mexican oregano

1 tablespoon granulated garlic

1 tablespoon onion powder

2 tablespoons sea salt

1 tablespoon black pepper

DIRECTIONS

Combine the enchilada sauce, chili powder, paprika, cumin, coriander, oregano, granulated garlic, onion powder, salt, and pepper in a bowl and whisk until well mixed. Spoon into an airtight jar. Let stand for 12 hours to maximize flavor. May store in the refrigerator for up to 1 week.

RED MEAT
OIL MARINADE

Prep Time: 5 to 10 minutes   **Difficulty:** Easy   **Seasons:** 10 to 12 pounds

INGREDIENTS

5 cloves garlic

1 shallot

2 tablespoons Dijon mustard

2 tablespoons ground coriander seed

2 tablespoons chopped fresh rosemary

1 tablespoon chopped fresh thyme

4 teaspoons sea salt

2 tablespoons medium-ground black pepper

½ cup extra-virgin olive oil

DIRECTIONS

Peel the garlic. Press through a garlic press to mince finely or chop with a knife. Peel the shallot and chop finely. Combine the garlic and shallot in a bowl. Add the mustard, coriander seed, rosemary, thyme, salt and pepper. Add the olive oil in a slow drizzle, whisking constantly. Whisk until well blended. May store in an airtight container in the refrigerator for up to 1 week.

NOTE

I like to add just enough salt to this recipe to add flavor to the meat. I always finish seasoning the steak with sea salt once removed from the grill and resting in order to accent the rub and steak flavor.

SWEET CHILI
PICKLED RED ONIONS

Prep Time: 10 minutes (plus 24 hours)   **Difficulty:** Easy   **Yield:** 2 cups

---

INGREDIENTS

1 cup sherry vinegar

5 tablespoons sugar

1 tablespoon garlic chili paste

8 to 10 allspice berries

1 teaspoon kosher salt

2 red onions, cut into ¼-inch strips

DIRECTIONS Combine the vinegar, sugar, chili paste, allspice berries, and salt in a saucepan. Bring to a simmer over medium-high heat, stirring frequently. Cook until sugar and salt are dissolved, stirring frequently. Add the onions. Cook for 1 minute, stirring constantly; cover. Turn off the heat. Let stand for 10 minutes. Stir to mix well. Let stand for 10 minutes. Remove to a large lidded jar. Chill for 24 hours before serving. May store, tightly covered, in the refrigerator for 10 to 12 days.

NOTE *For use in dips, sides, garnishes, or on their own, these flavor-packed onions take only 24 hours to marinate in garlic chili and keep for nearly two weeks. Do you have a picnic or party planned this weekend? Enhance almost any dish with these delicious onions. They're well worth the 10 minutes they take to prepare.*

TOMATO
PICCALILLI

Prep Time: 1 hour (plus 8 to 10 hours)   **Difficulty:** Medium   **Yield:** 4 cups

INGREDIENTS

6 green tomatoes, stemmed

6 tomatillos

1 head green cabbage, shredded

2 medium yellow onions, finely chopped

3 green bell peppers, finely chopped

¼ cup sea salt

3 cups distilled vinegar

1½ cups packed brown sugar

3 tablespoons pickling spices

1 cinnamon stick

DIRECTIONS

Cut the tomatoes into ¼-inch pieces. Remove the papery coverings and stems from the tomatillos using a knife. Cut the tomatillos into ¼-inch pieces. Chop the cabbage finely.

Combine the tomatoes, tomatillos, cabbage, onions, and bell peppers in a large bowl. Add the salt and toss to mix. Chill for 8 to 10 hours. Strain in a mesh strainer or cheesecloth-lined colander, pressing to release all of the liquid.

Combine the vinegar, brown sugar, pickling spices, and cinnamon stick in a large saucepan. Add the vegetables; cover. Bring to a simmer over medium-low heat. Simmer for 30 to 45 minutes or until the liquid is reduced, stirring occasionally and reducing the heat if needed to prevent burning. Discard the cinnamon stick. Spoon into a container; cover. Let stand to cool. May store at room temperature or in the refrigerator for up to 8 days.

NOTE

Since this relish is typically made with green tomatoes, blending in tomatillos adds a bright acidic kick.

CAROLINA
SAUCE

Prep Time: 5 minutes   **Difficulty:** Easy   **Yield:** 2 cups

INGREDIENTS	1 cup Dickey's Original Barbecue Sauce	¼ cup dill pickle juice (not bread and butter)
	½ cup yellow mustard	1 tablespoon Louisiana-style hot sauce

DIRECTIONS Combine the Dickey's Original Barbecue Sauce, mustard, pickle juice and hot sauce in a small saucepan. Cook until heated through. Serve warm with pulled pork, pork ribs, or pork steaks.

NOTE *Pork has found its way into Texas barbecue. While our Texas-style sauce tastes great on pork steaks and pulled pork, this classic, vinegar-based Carolina sauce showcases the flavor of smoked pork. This is our nod to South Carolina barbecue sauce.*

Warren Dickey's
FAVORITE
MEAT SAUCE

Prep Time: 2 hours   **Difficulty:** Easy   **Serves:** 4 to 6

INGREDIENTS

1½ tablespoons extra-virgin olive oil

1 tablespoon unsalted butter

1 pound 90/10 ground beef

½ yellow onion, finely chopped

2 cloves garlic, minced

2 cups chicken stock

1 cup whole milk

1 (8-ounce) can tomato sauce

1 teaspoon red chili flakes

⅓ teaspoon ground black pepper

2 tablespoons chopped Italian parsley

½ teaspoon kosher salt, or to taste

DIRECTIONS

Heat the olive oil and butter in a saucepan over high heat until the butter is melted. Add the ground beef. Cook for 5 to 7 minutes or until brown, stirring to crumble. Reduce the heat to medium. Add the onion and garlic. Cook just until the color changes. Add the stock, milk, tomato sauce, chili flakes, and pepper. Bring to a boil over medium-high heat. Stir the sauce to mix well. Reduce the heat to low. Cook, covered, for 1½ hours, stirring every 20 minutes. Cook, uncovered, for 20 minutes or until reduced, stirring frequently. Remove from the heat. Stir in the parsley and salt. Adjust the pepper to taste.

> *Warren is a seven-year-old who's learning to cook and knows what he likes. Warren likes this dish so much that it's become a weekly standard over at the Dickey household. Our meat sauce usually begins its life on pasta and then the leftovers make a secondary appearance later in the week as the star ingredient for sloppy joes."*

DR PEPPER®
BARBECUE SAUCE

Prep Time: 30 minutes   **Difficulty:** Medium   **Yield:** 2 cups

---

INGREDIENTS

2 tablespoons unsalted butter

1 medium yellow onion, chopped

3 cloves garlic, minced

½ cup ketchup

6 tablespoons tomato paste

½ cup packed dark brown sugar

½ cup apple cider vinegar

¼ cup Worcestershire sauce

2 teaspoons chili powder

½ teaspoon ground cumin

½ teaspoon medium-ground black pepper

¼ teaspoon cayenne pepper

1 (12-ounce) can Dr Pepper

1 teaspoon lime juice

1 teaspoon kosher salt, or to taste

DIRECTIONS

Melt the butter in a small saucepan over medium heat. Cook the onion and garlic in the butter for 6 to 8 minutes or until translucent; do not brown. Add the ketchup, tomato paste, brown sugar, vinegar, Worcestershire sauce, chili powder, cumin, black pepper, cayenne pepper and Dr Pepper and mix well. Simmer over medium-low heat for 20 minutes, stirring occasionally. Let stand to cool for 15 minutes. Add the lime juice and salt and process in a blender or with an immersion blender until smooth.

NOTE

Dickey's and Dr Pepper are rooted in Texas history. Why not combine both to make a perfect, Texas-style barbecue sauce? Adding lime juice at the end gives this sauce a fresh, bold kick.

THE SECRET IS IN THE SAUCE

It took three years, two fist fights, and a kitchen fire before we perfected the sauce that Dickey's serves today. A unique blend of secret spices gives our original barbecue sauce a tangy, smoky, and wonderfully memorable flavor. Sometime in 1972, Roland, Sr., perfected the Dickey's sauce recipe in the back of the original location, and it's very close to what we manufacture today. In the barbecue business, your sauce is just as important as the meats you're loading in and out of the smoker. After years of struggling to maintain consistency and quality when there was a tomato shortage with outside sauce manufacturers, we decided to make our own Dickey's sauce. This decision led to the founding of Wycliff Douglas Foods, Inc.

"Barbecue should be great with or without sauce, but the sauce is what makes it unique. Folks remember great sauce. We built Wycliff Douglas to protect the family sauce recipe. We had to make sure our sauce is always consistent and uniquely Dickey's," says Roland Dickey, Jr.

Nick Schwabe and Roland Dickey, Jr., have been best friends since high school. They came up with an unorthodox housing plan and purchased a fourplex apartment they occupied at the corners of Wycliff and Douglas in college and lease out the other two units to cover their mortgage. Years later, when it was time to sell, they made a nice profit. This capital was the beginning seed money that launched Wycliff Douglas Foods. Today, the company makes not only Dickey's signature barbecue sauces, spices, and rubs but also private-label products for other restaurant companies. They have also protected the original barbecue sauce recipe and expanded to six varieties of sauces.

Wycliff Douglas Foods, Inc., staff

Roland, Jr., Laura Rea, and Nick Schwabe

BROWN SUGAR WHISKEY
MOP SAUCE

Prep Time: 15 minutes   **Difficulty:** Easy   **Yield:** 2½ cups

---

INGREDIENTS

½ cup salted butter

½ yellow onion, finely chopped

1 cup apple cider vinegar

½ cup pineapple juice

Grated zest and juice of 1 lemon

3 tablespoons packed dark brown sugar

½ teaspoon ground black pepper

1 cup Texas whiskey

DIRECTIONS

Melt the butter in a saucepan over medium-high heat. Add the onion and cook until translucent, stirring frequently; do not brown. Add the vinegar, pineapple juice, lemon zest, lemon juice, brown sugar, and pepper and mix well. Bring to a low boil. Simmer over medium-low heat for 5 to 6 minutes or until slightly reduced. Remove from the heat. Add the whiskey and mix well. Keep at 145 degrees if using immediately. Reheat the sauce before using if the sauce has cooled. May store in the refrigerator for up to 1 week.

VINEGAR
MOP SAUCE

Prep Time: 5 minutes   **Difficulty:** Easy   **Yield:** 2½ cups

INGREDIENTS

½ yellow onion

¼ cup chopped fresh cilantro

3 serrano peppers, seeded and stemmed

2 cups apple cider vinegar

¼ cup water

2 tablespoons Asian chili garlic sauce

1 tablespoon sea salt

1 teaspoon freshly ground black pepper

DIRECTIONS

Combine the onion, cilantro, serrano peppers, vinegar, water, chili garlic sauce, salt, and pepper in a blender. Process until puréed. Pour into a pitcher. Apply to barbecue using a string mop or large brush. Keep at 145 degrees if using immediately. Reheat the sauce before using if the sauce has cooled. May store in the refrigerator for up to 3 days.

NOTE

This classic mop sauces is used for long, slow barbecuing processes. It's great for pork, skirt steak, lamb, and even fish.

COMEBACK
SAUCE

Prep Time: 5 to 8 minutes   **Difficulty:** Easy   **Yield:** 1¾ cups

INGREDIENTS

1 cup mayonnaise

¼ cup Asian chili garlic sauce

¼ cup ketchup

2 teaspoons lemon juice

2 teaspoons Worcestershire sauce

1 teaspoon dry yellow mustard

½ teaspoon ground black pepper

DIRECTIONS

Combine the mayonnaise, chili garlic sauce, ketchup, lemon juice, Worcestershire sauce, dry mustard, and pepper in a bowl and whisk until well blended. May store in an airtight container for up to 1 week.

NOTE

This is a great dip for everything! From anything fried to grilled chicken (great twist to an Alabama white sauce) and even on a smoked prime rib in place of horseradish sauce.

ROASTED PEPPER
STEAK SAUCE

Prep Time: 40 minutes   **Difficulty:** Medium   **Yield:** 1½ cups

INGREDIENTS

1 red bell pepper

1 orange

½ yellow onion, chopped

4 cloves garlic, minced

1 cup white wine

1 cup balsamic vinegar

½ cup ketchup

½ cup Worcestershire sauce

½ cup Dijon mustard

½ cup golden raisins

1 teaspoon celery salt

1 teaspoon hot paprika

1 teaspoon ground black pepper

1 teaspoon kosher salt

DIRECTIONS

Preheat the broiler or grill to high. Broil or grill the bell pepper on the rack until charred, turning frequently. Place the bell pepper in a small bowl and cover with plastic wrap. Let stand for 5 to 10 minutes or until the skin loosens. Stem the pepper and remove the skin and seeds. Chop the pepper into 1-inch pieces.

Peel the orange using a vegetable peeler. Place the orange peel in a saucepan. Juice the orange and add the juice to the peel. Add the bell pepper, onion, garlic, wine, vinegar, ketchup, Worcestershire sauce, mustard, raisins, celery salt, paprika, black pepper, and salt and mix well. Simmer over low heat for 20 to 25 minutes or until the sauce is thickened and adheres to the back of the spoon, stirring frequently. Remove the orange peels. Strain the sauce, using the back of the spoon to break down any large pieces; sauce should be smooth. Pour into a glass jar or airtight container. Let stand to cool before serving.

BUTTERMILK
RANCH DRESSING

Prep Time: 10 minutes   **Difficulty:** Easy   **Yield:** 1½ cups

INGREDIENTS

1 teaspoon dried parsley

1 teaspoon dried dill

½ teaspoon dried chives

½ teaspoon onion powder

½ teaspoon granulated garlic

½ teaspoon sea salt

¼ teaspoon freshly ground black pepper

½ cup mayonnaise

½ cup sour cream or plain Greek yogurt

½ cup buttermilk

Grated zest and juice of ½ lemon

½ teaspoon Worcestershire sauce

DIRECTIONS

Combine the parsley, dill, chives, onion powder, granulated garlic, salt, and pepper in a bowl and crush lightly with the back of a spoon. Add the mayonnaise, sour cream, buttermilk, lemon zest, lemon juice, and Worcestershire sauce and whisk until smooth. Pour into a lidded jar or airtight container. Chill until serving time. May store in the refrigerator for up to 7 days.

NOTE

You can use fresh parsley for this recipe, but we prefer the remaining herbs to be dried. Too many fresh herbs in a ranch dressing can make it taste grassy.

RANCH DRESSING, RESERVATIONS, & THE ART OF REPLATING

It is somewhat ironic that Laura Rea Dickey, CEO of Dickey's Barbecue Pit Restaurants, Inc., can't necessarily cook. She is highly accomplished, however, at making reservations, martinis, and of all things, ranch dressing. She's also a rare talent in the art of replating. Not long after graduating from college, the company Laura was working for announced they would have a potluck dinner for their annual Christmas party. Panicked, she called her father, Dennis Rea, for help and his famous lasagna recipe.

"Here's what you'll do," he said. "You'll pick up a Stouffer's® lasagna, bake it, replate it in a nice Pyrex dish, and add some fresh ricotta and Parmesan cheese. Well, it's you so get two, and the second one will probably be ok. It would be bad form to give your new boss and coworkers food poisoning, so you need to excel in the art of replating."

"Ok, I can do that," Laura responded. "Wait, is that your famous lasagna recipe too? Or is this just to compensate for me not being able to even boil an egg?"

"Let's just say replating and making excellent restaurant reservations is a Rea family tradition. When you're ready, I will teach you my one real recipe, homemade ranch dressing, but you need to excel at replating first." Armed with her father's advice, Laura's homemade lasagna was a huge hit. She has since matriculated to actually making homemade ranch dressing and a great dirty martini and has perfected the art of reservations and replating.

Dennis and Sandy Rea on their wedding day

Dennis, Laura, and Sandy Rea at Laura's high school graduation

GREEN GODDESS
DRESSING

Prep Time: 8 to 10 minutes   **Difficulty:** Medium   **Yield:** 1½ cups

INGREDIENTS

1 cup chopped fresh curly parsley

¼ cup chopped fresh cilantro

¼ cup chopped fresh mint

2 tablespoons chopped chives

2 tablespoons chopped fresh tarragon

1 tablespoon small capers

½ cup plain Greek yogurt

½ cup mayonnaise

2 tablespoons lemon juice

1 teaspoon Dijon mustard

1 clove garlic, peeled

1 teaspoon sea salt

½ teaspoon freshly ground black pepper

DIRECTIONS

Process the parsley, cilantro, mint, chives, tarragon, capers, yogurt, mayonnaise, lemon juice, mustard, garlic, salt, and pepper in a food processor for a dressing with chopped herbs or a blender for a smooth dressing. Pour into a lidded jar or airtight container. Chill until serving time. May store in the refrigerator for up to 5 to 6 days.

NOTE

Depending on your ingredients and how you plan to use this dressing, adjust the ratios of Greek yogurt to mayonnaise in this recipe. If you are using as a salad dressing, vegetable dip, or poultry sauce, use more yogurt. If using with red meats or on a fried chicken sandwich, use more mayonnaise to make the sauce richer.

Mrs. Dickey's
ITALIAN
DRESSING

Prep Time: 5 minutes   **Difficulty:** Easy   **Yield:** 1½ cups

INGREDIENTS

⅓ cup red wine vinegar

1 tablespoon Italian seasoning

1 tablespoon Worcestershire sauce

¼ teaspoon kosher salt

¼ teaspoon black pepper

1 cup extra-virgin olive oil

DIRECTIONS

Combine the vinegar, Italian seasoning, Worcestershire sauce, salt, and pepper in a bowl and whisk to mix. Add the olive oil gradually, whisking constantly until well mixed and smooth.

SIMPLE CITRUS
VINAIGRETTE

Prep Time: 5 minutes   **Difficulty:** Easy   **Yield:** 1 cup

INGREDIENTS

¼ cup fresh lemon juice

2 tablespoons honey

2 tablespoons apple cider vinegar

1 tablespoon Creole mustard

1 teaspoon sea salt

½ cup light olive oil

DIRECTIONS

Combine the lemon juice, honey, vinegar, mustard and salt in a bowl or blender. Add the olive oil gradually, whisking or processing constantly. Whisk or process until smooth and well blended. Pour into a lidded jar or airtight container. May store in the refrigerator for up to 2 weeks. Shake well before using.

NOTE

This dressing can be stored at room temperature or refrigerated.

SIDES
&VEGGIES

Kristin Peterson's
GRILLING
FRUITS

Grilling fruits is fun, and there are no boundaries.

Grill whatever is seasonal and flavor with whatever you like. It can be complementary or something new and strange; no one is judging. Fruits can be grilled directly over the coals or open flame. Just be careful because they contain sugar, which will burn quickly if unattended. It's okay to flip them to ensure the fruits are not burning. The grill temperature should be 350 to 400 degrees. Charcoal or wood can be a hardwood or fruitwood. I would stay away from mesquite because it is too strong for most fruits. Using a spatula and tongs to place and flip fruits on the grill works great together.

BEST WAY TO TRIM & CUT FRUITS SO THEY CAN BE GRILLED AND NOT LOST TO THE COALS

- **Watermelon:** 1-inch-thick wedges with rind on

- **Mango:** Halved with pit removed and crosscut but kept intact on skin

- **Apricots:** Halved with pits removed

- **Plums and Peaches:** Halved with pits removed

- **Bananas:** Peeled and halved lengthwise

- **Pineapple:** ½-inch-thick wedges with rind on

- **Kiwi:** Ends trimmed, peeled with a sharp knife, and crosscut into ½-inch slices

- **Lemons and Limes:** Halved with small ends removed

- **Apples:** Halved and sliced ¼ inch thick with seeds removed

- **Strawberries:** Halved with stems removed

SEASONING & SERVING IDEAS

- **Watermelon:** Season with salt and pepper, grill for 2 minutes on each side, and then brush with some Texas whiskey after you take them off the grill. Also take a sip for yourself. These are great to snack on.

- **Mango and Apricots:** Season with Nashville hot spice or cayenne pepper and grill for 3 to 4 minutes on the cut side; remove skin before serving. Serve with fried chicken in place of pickles.

- **Peaches, Plums, or Bananas:** Season with a little 5-spice and grill on both sides for 3 to 4 minutes. Serve with a scoop of vanilla ice cream.

- **Pineapple or Kiwi:** Season with Dickey's Rib Rub and grill. Chop and serve on pulled pork or fish tacos.

- **Lemons and Limes:** Season with salt and pepper and grill. Serve with grilled fish or even steak.

- **Apples and Strawberries:** Season with black pepper and added to a summer salad with toasted walnuts and blue cheese. Or serve over ice cream with caramel sauce.

Grill fruit over direct heat to cook quickly and impart flavor and texture. The fruit can be served immediately or cooled down and made into a salad.

> *Grilled fruits are my favorite healthy dessert option at a barbecue. It's smoky yet light, and it tastes like summer.*

Pit Master Joan Dahl's
SASSY
CRANBERRIES

Prep Time: 30 minutes (plus 8 hours) **Difficulty:** Easy **Serves:** 4 to 6

INGREDIENTS

¾ cup water

2 cups sugar

½ cup port wine

4 cups fresh cranberries, washed

⅓ cup orange liqueur, preferably Grand Marnier

DIRECTIONS

Combine the water, sugar, and port wine in a 3-quart saucepan and stir until blended. Add the cranberries. Bring to a boil over medium to high heat. Boil for 7 to 9 minutes or until the skins are cracked, stirring frequently. Let stand to cool for 10 to 15 minutes.

Pour the mixture into a blender or food processor. Pulse until of the desired consistency. Spoon into a bowl. Add the Grand Marnier and mix well. Chill for 8 hours or more before serving.

> " *These are so delicious and are easy to double if you have a larger crowd.*"

CHEDDAR
GRITS

Prep Time: 25 minutes   **Difficulty:** Easy   **Serves:** 6 to 8

INGREDIENTS

4 cups whole milk

1 cup stone-ground white grits (not instant)

1 teaspoon kosher salt

2 tablespoons unsalted butter, cut into cubes

¼ cup half-and-half

1 cup shredded mild Cheddar cheese

1 cup shredded sharp Cheddar cheese

2 egg yolks (optional)

Cracked black pepper to taste

DIRECTIONS

Bring the milk just to a boil in a heavy-bottom saucepan over medium-high heat. Whisk in the grits until the grains are separated; cover. Reduce the heat to medium-low. Simmer for 10 minutes. Stir in the salt. Cook, covered, for 5 to 10 minutes or until the grits are tender. Add the butter, stirring constantly with a spoon. Add the half-and-half, mild Cheddar cheese, and sharp Cheddar cheese and mix until smooth. Remove from the heat. Stir in the egg yolks. Season with pepper.

NOTE

Remember the scene from My Cousin Vinny? *No, not the "two yutes," but the scene that talks about no proper southerner would ever cook instant grits? This is actually true, because there is nothing as satisfying with a fried egg than classic stone-ground white-corn grits. The large-ground grit texture and creaminess offset each other enough to let you know you're not eating porridge.*

Jay Rooney's
JALAPEÑO CHEDDAR
CORN BREAD

Prep Time: 35 minutes   **Difficulty:** Medium   **Serves:** 6 to 8

INGREDIENTS

3 tablespoons unsalted butter, softened

4 ounces cream cheese, softened

⅓ cup sugar

2 large eggs

½ cup whole milk

1 package corn muffin mix

½ cup frozen corn kernels, thawed and drained

1 jalapeño pepper, seeded and minced

3 tablespoons chopped cilantro

½ cup coarsely shredded Cheddar cheese

DIRECTIONS

Preheat the smoker, grill, or oven to 350 degrees. Grease a 10-inch skillet with a small amount of the butter.

Cream the cream cheese, remaining butter, and sugar in a mixing bowl until smooth. Add the eggs one at a time, beating constantly. Add the milk gradually, beating constantly. Add the corn muffin mix. Beat at low speed until smooth. Add the corn, jalapeño, and cilantro and stir to mix. Spoon into the prepared skillet. Sprinkle with the Cheddar cheese. Smoke for 25 minutes or until a wooden pick inserted near the center of the corn bread comes out clean.

> **"** *This recipe is always a huge hit for parties and family get-togethers. I suggest pairing the corn bread with some homemade chili when you want to add some spice."*

Pit Master Wendy Williams'
SMOKY JALAPEÑO
MAC & CHEESE

Prep Time: 1 hour, 10 minutes   **Difficulty:** Medium   **Serves:** 4 to 6

INGREDIENTS

2½ cups sour cream

1 (10-ounce) can cream of chicken soup

6 ounces Velveeta cheese, cut into cubes

6 ounces non-waxed Gouda cheese, cut into cubes

6 ounces Swiss cheese, cut into cubes

1 pound Dickey's Smoked Jalapeño Cheddar Sausage, cut into ½-inch pieces

1 tablespoon spicy brown mustard

½ teaspoon garlic powder

¼ teaspoon ground black pepper

1 sleeve butter crackers, crushed

2 tablespoons butter, melted

½ teaspoon kosher salt

½ teaspoon freshly cracked black pepper

16 ounces elbow macaroni, preferably Barilla

DIRECTIONS

Preheat the oven to 350 degrees. Butter a 9x13-inch baking dish. Combine the sour cream, soup, Velveeta cheese, Gouda cheese, Swiss cheese, Dickey's Smoked Jalapeño Cheddar Sausage, mustard, garlic powder, and ground black pepper in a large bowl and mix well. Combine the crackers, butter, salt, and cracked black pepper in a bowl and mix well.

Combine the macaroni and 4 to 6 quarts water in a large saucepan. Bring to a boil. Boil for just 3 or 4 minutes; drain. Add the macaroni to the sour cream mixture and mix well. Spoon into the prepared baking dish. Bake for 25 minutes; stir to mix well. Sprinkle with the cracker mixture. Bake for 25 minutes or until hot and bubbly and golden brown.

> *If you are ready to become a backyard barbecue hero, this Smoky Jalapeño Mac & Cheese is over-the-top delicious. Loaded with Dickey's Jalapeño Cheddar Sausage and extra cheese before getting a tender kiss of hardwood smoke."*

JALAPEÑO BEANS
WITH COTIJA

Prep Time: 15 minutes   **Difficulty:** Easy   **Serves:** 4 to 5

INGREDIENTS

1 (16-ounce) can Dickey's Jalapeño Barbecue Beans

2 ounces cotija cheese, crumbled

4 sprigs of cilantro, coarsely chopped (optional)

DIRECTIONS

Cook the Dickey's Jalapeño Barbecue Beans in a large saucepan over medium heat for 8 to 10 minutes or until heated to 165 degrees. Pour into a serving bowl. Sprinkle with the cotija cheese and cilantro.

Pit Master MJ Breaux's
RED BEANS
& RICE

Prep Time: 2½ hours (plus overnight) **Difficulty:** Easy **Serves:** 6 to 8

INGREDIENTS

4 tablespoons unsalted butter

1 medium onion, chopped

1 green bell pepper, chopped

3 ribs celery, finely chopped

4 cloves garlic, minced

1 pound dried red beans, rinsed and soaked overnight

2 quarts chicken stock

3 bay leaves

1 tablespoon Cajun seasoning

1 tablespoon kosher salt

2 teaspoons ground black pepper

2 teaspoons Italian seasoning

1 pound pulled pork

Long grain white rice

1 pound Dickey's Polish Sausage, cut into slices

Chopped fresh parsley, for garnish

> 66 *A southern classic! Rarely a week goes by that we don't have Red Beans and Rice. Given my family's love affair with all things Cajun, this recipe is a staple around my home.*"

DIRECTIONS Melt the butter in a large Dutch oven or stockpot over medium-high heat. Add the onion, bell pepper, and celery. Cook for 6 to 8 minutes or until the onion and celery are semi-translucent and the bell pepper is tender, stirring frequently. Add the garlic. Cook for 1 to 2 minutes, stirring constantly. Add the beans, chicken stock, bay leaves, Cajun seasoning, salt, black pepper, and Italian seasoning. Increase the heat to high. Bring to a boil, stirring frequently. Decrease the heat to medium-low. Simmer, covered, for 1½ hours, stirring every 20 to 30 minutes; uncover.

Increase the heat to medium. Bring the mixture to a simmer. Discard the bay leaves. Cook for 30 minutes or until the beans are tender and the sauce is of the desired consistency, mashing some of the beans with the back of a wooden spoon if the beans are too runny. Stir in the pulled pork. Cook over low heat for 15 minutes. Adjust salt and pepper.

Prepare the rice according to the package directions 30 minutes before serving time. Serve the beans over the rice. Top with Dickey's Polish Sausage and garnish with parsley.

Roland Dickey, Jr.'s
ROASTED
CAULIFLOWER

Prep Time: 45 minutes   **Difficulty:** Easy   **Serves:** 4

INGREDIENTS

1 large head cauliflower

2 tablespoons (or more) extra-virgin olive oil

¼ teaspoon fine sea salt

Freshly ground black pepper to taste

DIRECTIONS

Preheat the oven to 425 degrees. Line a large rimmed baking sheet with foil. Cut the base off the cauliflower using a chef's knife. Cut the head into 4 wedges. Slice off just the inner cores, keeping the rest intact. Cut each wedge crosswise into ½-inch slices. Break apart any intact florets. Arrange the florets on the prepared baking sheet. Drizzle with 2 tablespoons of the olive oil. Sprinkle with the salt and pepper and toss to evenly distribute the ingredients and coat the cauliflower with olive oil, using up to 1 tablespoon additional olive oil only if needed. Spread the cauliflower in an even layer. Bake for 25 to 35 minutes or until the edges are dark golden brown, tossing halfway through the baking time.

" *Roasted cauliflower is potatoes without the carbs.*"

SMOKED
BAKED POTATOES

Prep Time: 1 hour, 35 minutes   **Difficulty:** Easy   **Serves:** 4

INGREDIENTS

4 large russet potatoes

¼ cup rendered smoked brisket fat or bacon fat

2 tablespoons kosher salt

1 tablespoon freshly ground black pepper

1 teaspoon granulated garlic

Cold salted butter, for serving

DIRECTIONS

Preheat a smoker or grill to 275 to 350 degrees. Wash the potatoes thoroughly and pat dry with paper towels. Rub the brisket fat over the surface of the potatoes. Combine the salt, pepper, and granulated garlic in a small bowl and crush with the back of a spoon. Season each potato with ¾ tablespoon of the mixture; do not wrap with foil. Grill or smoke the potatoes for 1½ hours or until easily pierced with a fork or skewer. Serve with butter. May serve with additional toppings if desired.

NOTE

I like to make baked potatoes anytime I am running my grill or smoke at 275 degrees for longer than 90 minutes. Why wouldn't you smoke more than one thing when you light the fire? You can go crazy with the toppings, but these potatoes are all about the smoky and salty skins, so keep it simple. If you do not have brisket or bacon fat, olive oil is a good substitute.

BACON-ROASTED
CAULIFLOWER

Prep Time: 40 to 50 minutes   **Difficulty:** Easy   **Serves:** 4 to 6

INGREDIENTS

1 head cauliflower

3 tablespoons Red Chili Rub
(recipe, page 82)

1 tablespoon olive oil

2 slices bacon

DIRECTIONS

Preheat the grill or oven to 325 degrees.

Cut the leaves and large stalk from the cauliflower, keeping the florets intact. Brush the top of the cauliflower with the Red Chili Rub and olive oil. Arrange the bacon in a crisscross pattern on top of the cauliflower. Place on a large piece of foil and fold the edges up to catch any drippings. Roast for 35 to 45 minutes or until the bacon has rendered and is crisp on the edges. Let stand for 5 minutes. Cut into 4 to 6 wedges.

Tricia Weir's
COLLARD
GREENS

Prep Time: 3 hours   **Difficulty:** Easy   **Serves:** 4 to 6

INGREDIENTS

1 (1½-pound) smoked ham hock

3 slices bacon

8 cups water

6 bunches collard greens, stemmed

½ yellow onion, chopped

2 tablespoons light brown sugar

1 tablespoon kosher salt

1 tablespoon chili garlic paste

1 tablespoon Worcestershire sauce

1 tablespoon apple cider vinegar

DIRECTIONS

Rinse the ham hock under warm running water for 10 to 20 seconds. Combine the ham hock, bacon, and water in a large stockpot. Cook, covered, over medium-high heat for 45 minutes or until the ham hock is fork-tender. Roll up a handful of greens at a time and cut into small pieces. Place the greens in a colander and wash a few times under cold running water, removing all sand, grit, and debris. Add the greens, onion, brown sugar, salt, chili garlic paste, Worcestershire sauce, and vinegar to the ham hock mixture, adding additional water if needed to cover the greens. Cook, covered, for 2 hours. Discard the bacon. Remove the ham hock to a cutting board. Debone the ham hock and chop and shred the meat, discarding any cartilage. Return the meat to the greens mixture and mix well.

NOTE

When buying collards, look for bright green and tender leaves. They should be able to pull away easily from the stem. To add a little kick to your greens, serve with additional cider vinegar and chili garlic paste on the side.

66 *Here's a quick tip. I will also add one diced turnip to my collards while cooking them. This adds a great flavor to the greens."*

Aunt Elizabeth's
CORN
DISH

Prep Time: 2¼ hours (plus 1 hour)   **Difficulty:** Easy   **Serves:** 8 to 10

INGREDIENTS

12 ears sweet yellow corn in the husk

Cold butter, for dish

6 tablespoons unsalted butter

3 tablespoons all-purpose flour

2 cups half-and-half

1 teaspoon kosher salt

1 teaspoon ground black pepper

½ teaspoon dried thyme

¼ cup chopped green onions

DIRECTIONS

Preheat the oven to 350 degrees. Arrange the corn on a baking sheet. Bake for 1 hour and turn off the oven. Let the corn stand in the husk to cool at room temperature for 1 hour. Shuck the corn and remove the silk. Cut the kernels from the corn using a sharp knife.

Preheat the oven to 350 degrees. Grease a baking dish with a small amount of cold butter. Melt the 6 tablespoons butter in a saucepan. Add the flour and mix until smooth to make a roux. Cook for 1 minute, stirring constantly; do not brown. Whisk in the half-and-half. Bring to a low boil. Cook for 24 to 26 minutes or until thickened, stirring constantly. Remove from the heat. Add the salt, pepper, thyme, and corn and mix well. Stir in the green onions. Spoon into the prepared baking dish. Bake for 40 minutes.

"For variety, I sometimes add 1 can of ranch-style beans that has been drained and rinsed. This gives it a quirky Tex-Mex flavor, even with the cream sauce—fold in before cooking. Other varieties include sprinkling the top with canned fried onions or grated cheese (cover with foil until the last 10 minutes) or folding in ½-inch slices of 1 can or jar of canned tamales before cooking the dish (they must be canned as fresh ones will not hold their shape)."

FIRST GRADE BUSINESSMAN

From the time he understood that their family name was on the front of the restaurant, Roland Dickey, Jr., learned to watch his dad's every move and wanted to make him proud. Right around first grade, Roland, Jr.'s teacher asked him why he chose to wear a suit jacket to school on Mondays even though some of the kids teased him about it.

"My dad wears a suit and says it's important to dress for success. He says successful men wear a 'suite hacket.' I want to be successful," Roland, Jr., told his teacher. Roland wore a suit jacket on Mondays throughout first grade.

At the age of eight, Roland, Jr., also wanted to build a business "like his dad did" and didn't see why he needed to wait. With the allowance he had saved, Roland purchased a Radio Flyer Red Wagon®. This, it turned out, was not just for fun but also for a business model that might be considered a "food truck" these days. In answer to his mother's protests, he reminded her that he was allowed to spend his hard-earned money on anything he wanted.

By himself, Roland walked to the neighborhood 7-Eleven® and worked out a wholesale agreement with the manager. With what he had left of his allowance, he purchased a variety of candy, loaded up his wagon, and set off to sell his inventory to classmates at the school bus stop—for a reasonable profit, of course, due to convenience and timing. Thinking ahead to theft prevention, he also carried a can of his mother's Aqua Net® hairspray for protection. This lucrative business went on for a few glorious months, all the while making Roland more and more money, until his mother and father were called to the principal's office. Sure enough, an older kid had tried to rob Roland of his cash box but was deterred with a blast of Aqua Net to the face. Regardless of the fact that he had to shut down his business at the behest of his principal and parents, Roland learned his first lesson in business: "Take what you have, and with hard work and ingenuity, find a way to turn your assets into profit." And, of course, keep a can of Aqua Net handy.

Roland, Jr., and Roland, Sr., food demo television segment

Roland, Jr., as a child

SMOKED OR ROASTED ELOTES

Prep Time: 30 to 60 minutes (plus 40 minutes)   **Difficulty:** Easy   **Serves:** 4 to 5

INGREDIENTS

5 ears sweet corn in husks

¼ cup mayonnaise

¼ cup crema Mexicana or sour cream

Juice of 1 small lime

2 to 4 teaspoons Valentina Mexican Hot Sauce

1 teaspoon Dickey's Rib Rub

⅓ cup crumbled cotija cheese or grated Parmesan cheese

4 sprigs of cilantro, torn

DIRECTIONS

Soak the corn in the husks in a large bowl of cold water for 30 minutes. Preheat a grill to 400 degrees or a smoker to 300 degrees using pecan pellets. Grill the corn for 30 minutes, turning every 8 to 10 minutes, or smoke the corn for 60 minutes. Remove to a tray. Let stand to cool for 5 to 10 minutes. Shuck the corn and remove the silk. Cut the kernels from the corn using a chef's knife and place in a baking dish.

Whisk the mayonnaise, crema Mexicana, and lime juice in a bowl until blended. Drop the mixture by spoonsful over the corn and mix well. Drizzle with the hot sauce. Keep warm in a 200-degree oven. Sprinkle with the Dickey's Rib Rub, cotija cheese, and cilantro just before serving.

CORNMEAL
FRIED OKRA

Prep Time: 15 minutes   **Difficulty:** Medium   **Serves:** 4 to 6

INGREDIENTS

1 pound fresh okra

¼ cup buttermilk

½ cup yellow cornmeal

½ cup all-purpose flour

1 teaspoon garlic salt

½ teaspoon black pepper

Vegetable oil, for frying

Dickey's Foo Foo Finishing Blend

DIRECTIONS

Rinse the okra with cold running water and pat dry with paper towels. Cut off and discard the stems. Cut the okra into 1-inch pieces.

Pour the buttermilk into a shallow bowl. Combine the cornmeal, flour, garlic salt, and pepper in a shallow bowl and mix well.

Dip the okra into the buttermilk to coat. Coat thoroughly with the cornmeal mixture.

Pour 1½ inches of vegetable oil into a medium saucepan. Heat over medium-high heat to 375 degrees or until shimmery.

Fry the okra in batches of 10 to 15 pieces for 2 minutes. Turn the okra over using a slotted spoon. Fry for 1½ to 2 minutes or until golden brown. Remove to paper towels to drain. Sprinkle with Dickey's Foo Foo Finishing Blend.

NOTE

Fresh okra is now available year-round. You can use frozen okra, but make sure to drain very well and pat dry with a paper towel to ensure the buttermilk does not get watered down and cause the breading not to stick.

Roland Dickey, Jr.'s
SPLIT
PEA SOUP

Prep Time: 70 minutes   **Difficulty:** Medium   **Serves:** 6 to 8

INGREDIENTS

8 ounces sliced bacon, chopped

1 large onion, chopped

2 ribs celery, sliced

16 ounces dried green split peas

2 quarts water

2 medium potatoes, peeled and diced

2 cups diced cooked ham

2 teaspoons salt

1 bay leaf

¼ teaspoon pepper

1 cup heavy whipping cream

DIRECTIONS Cook the bacon in a Dutch oven or soup kettle over medium heat until crisp. Remove to paper towels using a slotted spoon. Add the onion and celery to the drippings. Sauté until tender; drain the drippings from the Dutch oven. Add the peas, water, potatoes, ham, salt, bay leaf, and pepper and mix well. Bring to a boil. Reduce the heat to medium-low. Simmer, covered, for 45 minutes or until the peas are very tender, stirring occasionally. Discard the bay leaf. Pour the soup into a large bowl. Let cool for 20 minutes. Process in batches in a blender until smooth, returning to the Dutch oven. Stir in the cream. Cook over medium heat just until heated through; do not boil. Ladle into soup bowls and sprinkle servings with equal portions of the bacon.

" I'm obsessed with this soup. The texture is comparable to a creamy potato soup. With natural ingredients, it is very flavorful and healthy. It's one of my go-to recipes in the winter months for Laura and I."

Sherri Stoel's
BARBECUE GREEN BEAN
CASEROLE WITH BACON

Prep Time: 55 minutes   **Difficulty:** Easy   **Serves:** 6 to 7

HOME OFFICE GREATS

INGREDIENTS

8 ounces applewood- or cherrywood-smoked bacon

½ yellow onion, finely diced

1 red bell pepper, finely diced

1 (16-ounce) package frozen hash brown potatoes

1 (16-ounce) package frozen green beans, thawed

1 (16-ounce) can Dickey's Texas Barbecue Beans

1 cup Dickey's Original Barbecue Sauce

1 (2.8-ounce) can crispy fried onions

DIRECTIONS

Preheat a grill or smoker to 275 to 300 degrees using oak charcoal or fruitwood. Cut the bacon into ½-inch pieces. Cook the bacon in a large saucepan over medium heat until brown and crisp, stirring frequently. Drain half of the drippings from the skillet. Add the onion and bell pepper. Cook for 2 to 3 minutes or until the onion is tender. Add the potatoes, green beans, Dickey's Texas Barbecue Beans, and Dickey's Original Barbecue Sauce and mix with a spatula. Spoon into a baking pan. Grill or smoke the bean mixture for 40 to 45 minutes. Sprinkle with the fried onions and serve.

> 66 *You won't need any mushroom soup for this recipe because it's all about the barbecue.*

POTATOES
AU GRATIN

Prep Time: 55 minutes   **Difficulty:** Medium   **Serves:** 4 to 6

INGREDIENTS

4 russet potatoes

½ cup rendered duck fat or olive oil

1 teaspoon sea salt

½ cup diced yellow onion

½ cup diced green bell pepper

2 tablespoons unsalted butter

1 cup heavy cream

½ teaspoon ground black pepper

¼ cup shredded Cheddar cheese

2 tablespoons sliced green onions

DIRECTIONS

Preheat the oven to 425 degrees. Line a baking sheet with foil. Wash the potatoes thoroughly and pat dry with paper towels. Cut the potatoes into 1-inch cubes and place in a large bowl. Add the duck fat and toss to coat the potatoes. Spread on the prepared baking sheet. Roast for 20 to 25 minutes or until brown, stirring every 5 minutes. Sprinkle with the salt. Lift the potatoes with the foil and pour the potatoes into a large bowl.

Sauté the yellow onion and bell pepper in the butter in a sauté pan over medium heat for 5 minutes; do not brown. Add the cream and bring to a simmer. Remove from the heat. Whisk in the black pepper and Cheddar cheese until smooth. Pour over the potatoes and toss with a spatula. Spoon into a serving bowl and cover. Keep warm in a 175-degree oven for 20 minutes before serving. Sprinkle with the green onions.

NOTE

Typically Potatoes au Gratin differ from Scalloped Potatoes due to the crisp bread crumb topping. The twist to this recipe is to first crisp the potatoes until brown and then toss with the cheese sauce. Delicious!

Nick Schwabe's
SCALLOPED
POTATOES

HOME OFFICE GREATS ★

Prep Time: 45 to 60 minutes   **Difficulty:** Medium   **Serves:** 4 to 6

INGREDIENTS

4 cups thinly sliced peeled Yukon Gold or russet potatoes (about 2 pounds), divided

3 tablespoons butter

3 tablespoons all-purpose flour

1½ cups milk

1 teaspoon salt

Dash of cayenne pepper

1½ cups grated sharp Cheddar cheese, divided

Paprika to taste

DIRECTIONS

Preheat the oven or grill to 350 degrees. Grease a 1½-quart baking dish or cast-iron skillet. Spread half of the potatoes evenly in the prepared baking dish.

Melt the butter in a small saucepan over medium heat. Stir in the flour. Whisk in the milk, salt and cayenne pepper. Bring just to a boil over medium-low heat, stirring occasionally with a whisk until smooth. Reduce the heat to low. Stir in 1 cup of the Cheddar cheese. Pour half of the sauce over the potatoes in the baking dish. Add the remaining potatoes, spreading evenly. Add the remaining sauce. Sprinkle with the remaining ½ cup Cheddar cheese. Sprinkle with paprika. Bake or grill, loosely covered with foil, for 30 minutes. Bake, uncovered, for 15 to 20 minutes until the potatoes are fork-tender and the cheese is brown.

> 66 *My idea of the BEST Scalloped Potatoes! These are rich and creamy and have just the right amount of cheesy flavor. A staple side dish recipe that's perfect for weekends and holiday dinners.*"

SOUTHERN
WHIPPED POTATOES

Prep Time: 30 to 40 minutes   **Difficulty:** Easy   **Serves:** 6 to 8

INGREDIENTS

4 pounds russet potatoes, peeled

1 gallon cold tap water

½ cup unsalted butter

½ cup sour cream

½ cup heavy cream

1½ teaspoons kosher salt

¾ teaspoon ground black pepper

DIRECTIONS

Peel the potatoes and cut crosswise into 1-inch slices. Combine the potatoes and water in a stockpot. Bring to a boil over medium-high heat. Reduce the heat to medium. Cook the potatoes for 15 to 20 minutes or until fork-tender; drain in a colander or strainer. Let stand to steam in the colander for 5 minutes or until slightly drier.

Combine the butter, sour cream, and heavy cream in the stockpot. Cook over medium heat until the butter is melted and comes to a slight boil. Stir in the potatoes, salt, and pepper. Remove from the heat.

Beat the potatoes at medium speed with a hand mixer for 1 minute or to the desired smoothness; do not overmix. Serve warm.

Shannon Bullock's
TATER TOT
CASSEROLE

Prep Time: 1 hour   **Difficulty:** Medium   **Serves:** 8 to 10

INGREDIENTS

1 pound lean ground beef

½ yellow onion, finely diced

1 teaspoon granulated garlic

½ teaspoon ground black pepper

1 (10-ounce) can fiesta cheese soup

4 pounds frozen tater tots

1 (16-ounce) package frozen green beans, thawed

1 (10-ounce) can cream of mushroom soup

2 cups shredded Cheddar cheese

DIRECTIONS

Preheat the oven to 375 degrees. Grease an 8- or 9-inch cast-iron skillet lightly with butter. Brown the ground beef in a large skillet over medium-high heat, stirring to crumble; drain the drippings from the skillet. Add the onion, granulated garlic, and pepper. Sauté for 4 to 5 minutes or until the onion is tender. Add the fiesta cheese soup and stir to mix well.

Line the bottom of the prepared cast-iron skillet with half of the tater tots. Layer with the ground beef mixture, green beans, and cream of mushroom soup. Sprinkle with half of the Cheddar cheese. Add the remaining tater tots and sprinkle with the remaining Cheddar cheese. Bake for 40 to 45 minutes or until golden brown and the cheese is melted. Serve immediately.

66 *Please note: Two layers of tater tots are always better than one. Or, if you are like my daughter, she says to go for three!"*

ASIAGO
CREAMED SPINACH

Prep Time: 15 to 20 minutes   **Difficulty:** Medium   **Serves:** 3 to 4

INGREDIENTS

4 tablespoons unsalted butter

2 shallots, finely chopped

4 cloves garlic, minced

3 tablespoons all-purpose flour

1½ cups cold whole milk

½ cup heavy cream

⅛ teaspoon ground nutmeg

1 pound fresh large-leaf spinach

1 teaspoon kosher salt

¼ teaspoon freshly ground black pepper

½ cup grated asiago cheese or Parmesan cheese

DIRECTIONS

Melt the butter in a heavy-bottom saucepan over medium heat. Sauté the shallots and garlic in the butter until tender; do not brown. Whisk in the flour. Cook for 1 minute; do not brown. Whisk in the milk, cream, and nutmeg, increasing the heat to medium-high. Cook until the sauce is thickened, stirring occasionally. Reduce the heat to medium. Simmer the sauce for 2 to 3 minutes, stirring occasionally. Remove from the heat.

Rinse the spinach well and remove the stems. Place in a microwave-safe bowl. Microwave for 2 to 3 minutes or until the spinach is wilted. Remove to a colander or cheesecloth. Squeeze out any excess moisture. Cut into ½-inch strips on a cutting board.

Bring the sauce just to a boil over medium heat. Add the spinach, salt, and pepper. Cook and stir until well mixed. Stir in the asiago cheese. Serve immediately.

GRUBER, YOU'RE FIRED!

Jeff Gruber is a recovering attorney who has been fired more times from Dickey's than any other employee. "I always walk into a room and ask Gruber what he's doing. Then, I tell him that's terrible and that he's probably fired, and I leave. I always know who is new when that person is in the room, too, and is shocked when Gruber laughs and responds with, 'Thank you, Mr. Dickey, I wanted to leave early today,'" says Roland Dickey, Sr.

And by fired, we mean to say that Jeff Gruber has been with the company for thirteen years and has performed brilliantly in many key positions, so much so that he's been moved into new roles to establish them and then moved someplace else to take on another new challenge. Jeff is now our Senior Vice President of Franchise Administration, or at least, he was when this cookbook went to print.

Jeff Gruber, Aaron Brewer, and Laura Rea with Roland

Julie Moore's
SALTED COFFEE
SWEET POTATO FRIES

Prep Time: 35 minutes   **Difficulty:** Medium   **Serves:** 6 to 8

INGREDIENTS   2 pounds sweet potatoes   1 tablespoon Dickey's Salted Coffee Rub

2 tablespoons olive oil   1 tablespoon kosher salt

DIRECTIONS   Preheat the oven or grill to 475 degrees. Peel the sweet potatoes and cut lengthwise into ½-inch planks. Cut the planks lengthwise into ¼- to ½-inch sticks and place in a large bowl. Drizzle with the olive oil and toss to coat. Sprinkle with a mixture of the Dickey's Salted Coffee Rub and salt. Spread on a baking sheet, separating the sticks. Bake or grill on the second rack for 20 minutes. Turn the sweet potatoes over. Bake or grill for 10 minutes or until crisp and the edges are brown. May cook in an air fryer at 375 degrees for 20 minutes.

NOTE   *The salted coffee blends well with the sweetness of the sweet potatoes. Cooked in the oven or air fryer, they are a great option for a non-fried french fry.*

"This simple yet satisfying recipe is delicious! Using the Dickey's Salted Coffee Rub really transforms the dish."

Shannon Santos's
TOMATO, CHEDDAR, & BACON PIES

HOME OFFICE GREATS

Prep Time: 1 hour   **Difficulty:** Medium   **Serves:** 8

INGREDIENTS

8 slices bacon

1 (16-ounce) can Pillsbury Grands!® Flaky Layers Biscuits

4 heirloom tomatoes, cut into ¼-inch slices

½ teaspoon kosher salt

¼ teaspoon freshly ground black pepper

1¼ cups shredded sharp Cheddar cheese, divided

3 tablespoons grated Parmesan cheese

⅓ cup mayonnaise

1 egg, beaten

1 teaspoon dried dill

2 tablespoons thinly sliced green onions

1 teaspoon apple cider vinegar

1 teaspoon sugar

" *Simple and savory, this pie is a tasty addition to brunch buffets and leisurely luncheons.*"

DIRECTIONS

Cook the bacon in a skillet until brown and crisp. Remove to paper towels to drain; reserving the drippings. Grease 8 muffin cups with some of the reserved bacon drippings.

Press each biscuit into a 5½-inch circle and place each in a prepared muffin cup. Press the dough over the bottom and up the sides of the cups, forming a ¾-inch rim. Line each dough cup with a slice of bacon. Chill for 5 to 10 minutes.

Place the sliced tomatoes on paper towels. Season with the salt and pepper and let stand for 10 minutes. Pat the top of the slices with a paper towel. Cut each slice into quarters and fill the bottom third of each cup with tomatoes.

Preheat the oven to 375 degrees. Combine 1 cup of the Cheddar cheese, Parmesan cheese, mayonnaise, egg, dill, green onions, vinegar, and sugar in a bowl and mix with a spatula. Spoon 1 tablespoonful of the cheese mixture over the tomatoes in each muffin cup, pressing to flatten the tomatoes. Repeat the procedure with the remaining tomatoes and cheese mixture. Pull the edges of the dough over the filling, pleating and pinching the dough gently to hold in place. Brush the tops with a small amount of the reserved bacon drippings. Sprinkle with the remaining ¼ cup Cheddar cheese. Bake for 25 to 30 minutes or until the biscuits and cheese are golden brown. Let stand to cool in the pan for 3 to 4 minutes. Remove to a plate and serve.

NOTE

Using Pillsbury Grands!® Flaky Layers Biscuits is so much easier than making the crusts from scratch and saves some time.

MAINS
& ENTRÉES

'CUE TIPS, TRICKS, TOPICS, & BASICS

CHARCOAL VS. PELLET VS. STICK VS. GAS

There are not enough pages in this book to pontificate over which one is better. They all have a place, and understanding how to master any one of them can yield great products. The answer is whatever one fits on your patio, meets your time allowance, and meets your budget. Ultimately, you are outside harnessing the simple pleasure of fire and smoke. That's what we are all passionate about in this book!

TOOLS

This topic reminds me of the scene in *Tin Cup* when character Roy McAvoy is struggling with his golf game and dons a hoard of quick-fix gadgets to help his golf game. Keep it simple: good heavy tongs, spatula, wire brush, pepper mill, and thermometer. Now, here is the key: the length of any one of these tools depends on your sensitivity to heat. Just remember, the farther you move away, the harder it is to control your dexterity.

POULTRY

Most poultry, except duck or goose, typically benefits from a long marination or brine time. Anything more than 12 to 16 hours enhances the retention of natural juices when grilling, smoking, or even frying. Remember, adding sugar and salt to darker poultry cuts, like thighs or legs, will make them retain a pink color. Combat this with darker color mops or sauces on the outside of the meat to lessen the appearance of the pink color. If cooked to 165 degrees at the bone, the meat is fully cooked and safe to eat.

PORK

Let's break it into two types: lean vs. fatty. Lean cuts, like pork chops and tenderloins, should be handled like poultry: Marinades and brines help retain the natural juices and enhance flavor. Fattier cuts, like ribs, shoulder, and boneless country ribs, do not need to be brined or marinated. They can be seasoned and put onto the firepit or grill immediately. If left whole, they do require low and slow cooking to become tender.

FISH

Most firm-fleshed saltwater fish can be handled like a steak and will do extremely well directly over the coals on the grill. Cooking with highly flavorful woods, like mesquite and hickory, give most fish a bold flavor that pairs well with craft beers and wines. There are no boundaries on seasoning. Use dry seasonings, oil, wet marinades, or even brines to season or marinate steak-cut fish.

Freshwater fish are typically delicate and require much care. Keeping the fish whole aids in keeping it together while cooking directly over the coals. Cooking slower on an offset heat source can yield a great fillet, typically seasoned and grilled immediately vs. marinated.

BEEF *Let's break down temperatures.*

Rare steaks: Soft-textured steaks that will maintain an indent when pressed with finger or tongs and with a cool red interior—125-degree internal temperature

Medium-rare steaks: Steaks with a soft and springy feel and a warm red interior—130- to 135-degree internal temperature

Medium steaks: Steaks with a springy feel and a hot slightly red interior—135- to 145-degree internal temperature

Well-done steaks: Firm steaks with a hot interior void of any red—155- to 165-degree internal temperature

BEEF *Let's break down a few of the major cuts.*

Rib Eyes and Porterhouses: Rib eyes and porterhouses have more internal fat running through the muscle, making them great on the grill. Grill directly over the coal bed, but make sure to move if fat dripping off begins to create flare-ups. Seasoning, oil marinades, and wet marinades all work well with these cuts. These cuts benefit when cooked on the bone, which enhances the flavor greatly, but plan a little more cook time because the bone insulates the meat.

New York Strips, T-Bones, and Filets: These cuts are slightly leaner than other prime cuts and can suffer slightly from being grilled 100 percent. When grilling 100 percent of the way, the interior meat becomes dull in color and rough vs. shiny when cooked on a flattop or in a sauté pan with butter. The steaks also will be slightly tougher and dryer if cooked all the way on the grill. Using the grill to add an initial layer of flavor and finishing in a pan yields a beautiful piece of meat that is packed with flavor and will melt in your mouth. Cool smoke these steaks at 165 degrees for 10 to 20 minutes, depending on thickness. Remove from the grill and transfer to a hot cast-iron skillet with butter, crushed garlic cloves, black peppercorns, and fresh rosemary and thyme sprigs. Sear on each side, moving the steaks around to even out the crust before flipping. Cook to desired doneness. These cuts benefit when cooked on the bone, which enhances the flavor greatly, but plan a little more cook time because the bone insulates the meat.

Skirt Steaks, Flat-Iron Steaks, and Hanger Steaks: These steaks benefit from an oil marinade or liquid marinade. They absorb flavors and maintain them while cooking. Heat charcoal until it is evenly burnt and maintains a grill temperature of 400 degrees. Moving these steaks frequently during the cooking process will yield an even char on the exterior—not looking for grill marks. Skirt steak should typically be cooked slightly beyond medium-rare to aid in tenderizing the meat, while skirt steak and hanger steak benefit from being served medium-rare. All three of these steaks should be sliced across the grain to enhance tenderness. A sprinkle of freshly flaked sea salt on these steaks after resting makes their flavor pop.

Tri-Tips and Prime Ribs: Whole-muscle steaks like these do very well when reverse seared. Season them liberally and let marinate, uncovered, in the refrigerator for at least 4 hours prior to cooking. Cool smoke at 165 degrees for 40 to 90 minutes, depending on the size. The internal temperature should never be above 110 degrees during this process. Remove from the smoker and heat the smoker or grill to 375 to 450 degrees to sear. (This also can be done in an air fryer set to 395 degrees). Basting with melted butter helps brown the steak and adds flavor. Remove from the grill 4 to 6 degrees before desired doneness. These steaks will carryover cook when removed from the grill or smoker. Allow to rest 20 to 30 minutes prior to slicing. Serve as is or with natural juices and a dipping sauce.

BEEF
SHORT RIBS

Prep Time: 6 to 8 hours (plus overnight)　　**Difficulty:** Medium　　**Serves:** 4

INGREDIENTS

1 (4- to 5-pound) 4-bone beef short-rib plate, 2 inches thick

½ cup Red Chili Rub (recipe, page 82)

2 tablespoons kosher salt

2 tablespoons freshly ground black pepper

1 cup The Spritz (recipe, page 81)

4 tablespoons unsalted butter, melted

Pickles and sliced onions, for serving

DIRECTIONS

Trim the fat and silver skin from the meaty side of the beef short ribs. Remove the membrane from the bone side. Rub the ribs with the Red Chili Rub. Chill, covered, overnight.

Preheat the smoker to 275 degrees, preparing for indirect cooking using post oak wood pieces.

Mix the salt and pepper and season the short ribs on all sides. Place bone sides down on the smoker. Smoke for 2 hours. Add pecan and hickory wood pieces. Smoke for 2 to 3 hours or until a meat thermometer inserted in the thickest portion of the meat registers 185 degrees, spraying with The Spritz after 1 to 2 hours to prevent overdrying. Remove to a large piece of peach butcher paper or foil. Brush carefully with the butter and spray with The Spritz. Wrap with the paper.

Reduce the heat of the smoker to 225 to 250 degrees, adding oak pieces or charcoal. Place the wrapped ribs back in the smoker. Smoke for 3 hours until a meat thermometer inserted in the meat registers 201 to 203 degrees. Remove to a cooler. Let stand for 1 hour or longer to allow the ribs to rest and tenderize. Cut the ribs into 4 individual portions and arrange on a plate. Serve with pickles and onions.

NOTE   *The short-rib plate used for this recipe comes from the lower portion of the rib cage, known as the short plate. The short plate runs along the sixth to tenth rib and sits between the brisket cut in front of it and the flank steak cut behind it. They differ from beef back ribs, which are cut higher from the steer off of the prime rib. Please note, there is much less meat on a beef back rib.*

CAVE MAN
STEAK & POTATOES

Prep Time: 15 to 20 minutes (plus 70 minutes)   **Difficulty:** Medium   **Serves:** 2 to 4

INGREDIENTS

2 (14- to 18-ounce) bone-in Porterhouse steaks, at least 1¼ inches thick

4 teaspoons kosher salt

2 teaspoons freshly ground black pepper

2 Idaho russet potatoes

Flaked sea salt and freshly ground black pepper to taste

DIRECTIONS

Season each steak with 1 teaspoon kosher salt and ½ teaspoon pepper per side. Let stand at room temperature for 1 hour.

Rinse the potatoes thoroughly and wrap each in 2 layers of foil. Light lump charcoal or briquettes in a firepit or kettle-style grill; do not use lighter fluid or easy-lighting briquettes. Mound the lit coals high in the center of the firepit. Place the potatoes around the edge of the coals. Turn the potatoes every 10 minutes to prevent burning.

Spread out the hot coals in an even layer using a long-handled tool and wearing oven mitts.

Pat the steaks dry with a paper towel to remove any excess moisture. Fan the coals to blow off any loose ash. Place the steaks directly on the coals. Cook for 4 to 5 minutes per side. Remove to a wire rack and tent with foil. Let stand in a warm place for 10 minutes. Crush flaked sea salt and pepper evenly over the steaks.

Serve the steaks whole or remove the bone and slice the steak. Unwrap the potatoes and serve with desired toppings.

NOTE

Even though this process of cooking was popularized this century, it was a necessity at some point in history. There are two key pieces to this cooking style. First, fan the coals right before placing the steak over them. Secondly, pat the steak dry to reduce any moisture from the exterior of the steak. If you do both steps, you will not need to brush anything off the steak before eating. Also, use a bone-in steak, as it adds a lot of flavor when cooking.

Carissa De Santis's
REVERSE-SEARED
TRI-TIP STEAK

HOME OFFICE
GREATS

Prep Time: 60 to 80 minutes (plus 24 hours) **Difficulty:** Medium **Serves:** 6 to 8

INGREDIENTS

3 pounds tri-tip steak

4 tablespoons Red Meat Rub (recipe, page 79)

3 tablespoons unsalted butter, melted

2 teaspoons sea salt

1 recipe Comeback Sauce (recipe, page 94) or Roasted Pepper Steak Sauce (recipe, page 95)

DIRECTIONS

Trim the large areas of fat and silver skin from the steak 24 hours before cooking. Rub the steak evenly with the Red Meat Rub. Chill, covered, for 24 hours.

Preheat a pellet grill or wood-burning firepit to 200 degrees using hickory. Place the steak in the grill or firepit. Grill for 30 to 40 minutes or until a meat thermometer inserted into the thickest portion registers 110 degrees. Remove to a wire rack placed over a baking sheet.

Heat the grill or firepit to 450 to 500 degrees. Return the steak to the grill and brush with the butter. Grill until the steak is evenly charred and a meat thermometer inserted in the thickest portion registers 135 degrees for medium-rare or 150 degrees for well done, turning and brushing with butter every 5 minutes. Return the steak to the wire rack. Let stand to rest for 10 minutes.

Cut the steak across the grain into slices, changing the direction of the cuts where the grain changes. Sprinkle with the sea salt. Serve with the Comeback Sauce or Roasted Pepper Steak Sauce.

 Who doesn't love a reverse sear that adds a touch of smoke to give you that big flavor everyone loves? This reverse-seared tri-tip recipe is perfect for those summer nights hanging by the pool. Pair it with a great bottle of Petit Sirah, and you've got yourself a date night."

Mrs. Dickey's
SMOKED BRISKET
CHILI

Prep Time: 35 to 40 minutes   **Difficulty:** Easy   **Serves:** 6 to 8

INGREDIENTS

2 tablespoons olive oil

½ yellow onion, diced

1 (10-ounce) can diced tomatoes and green chilies, drained

1 chili kit

1 (8-ounce) can tomato sauce

2 cups water

1½ pounds smoked brisket, chopped

1 can Dickey's Jalapeño Beans or pinto beans (optional)

Corn chips, shredded sharp Cheddar cheese, sour cream, chopped green onions, pickled jalapeño peppers, and/or chopped cilantro, for topping

DIRECTIONS

Heat the olive oil in a medium saucepan over medium heat. Cook the onion in the oil until translucent, stirring frequently. Add the tomatoes and chili kit ingredients and mix well. Add the tomato sauce and water. Bring just to a simmer. Cook, covered, over medium-low heat for 15 minutes, stirring occasionally. Add the brisket and Dickey's Jalapeño Beans. Bring to a simmer over medium-low heat. Simmer for 5 to 8 minutes, stirring occasionally. Ladle into soup bowls and add toppings.

" Leftover brisket is the perfect, smoky chili meat. This dish can be made with beans or without."

WALKING
TACO

Prep Time: 5 to 10 minutes   **Difficulty:** Easy   **Serves:** 4

INGREDIENTS

4 individual-size bags Fritos® corn chips or tortilla chips

2 cups Poblano Queso (recipe, page 46), heated

2 cups Smoked Brisket Chili (recipe, page 146), heated

4 tablespoons finely diced red onion

4 tablespoons chopped fresh cilantro

1 or 2 green onions, thinly sliced

DIRECTIONS

Cut the top or one long side of each bag of chips and separate to make containers. Spoon ½ cup each Poblano Queso and Smoked Brisket Chili over the chips in each bag. Sprinkle each with 1 tablespoon onion, 1 tablespoon cilantro, and 3 or 4 jalapeño slices. May rinse the jalapeño slices in cold water 3 or 4 times to remove the seeds and oil for a milder taste. May spice up the flavor by adding thinly sliced jalapeño peppers.

Cullen Dickey's
BRISKET
MAC TACO

Prep Time: 7 to 8 minutes　　**Difficulty:** Easy　　**Serves:** 2

INGREDIENTS

8 ounces chopped cooked brisket

1½ cups mac and cheese

4 ounces barbecue sauce

4 (5-inch) flour tortillas

DIRECTIONS

Place the brisket in a microwave-safe bowl. Cover with a damp paper towel. Microwave on medium for 1 to 2 minutes or just until heated through. Place the mac and cheese in a microwave-safe bowl. Microwave, uncovered, on high just until heated through. Microwave the barbecue sauce on high in a microwave-safe bowl just until heated through.

Preheat a griddle or grill. Arrange the tortillas on the griddle. Cook just until warm; do not make crispy. Fill the tortillas with equal portions of the mac and cheese and brisket. Drizzle with the barbecue sauce. May add coleslaw for added crunch.

What to do with leftovers? Almost every day I see a post on what to do with barbecue leftovers. Try this quick-and-easy go-to recipe."

Jerry Murray's
SMOKED BRISKET
DIP SANDWICH

Prep Time: 2 hours   **Difficulty:** Easy   **Serves:** 6

INGREDIENTS

2 pounds brisket, smoked and sliced

½ cup salted butter

3 yellow onions, thinly sliced

2 cloves garlic, minced

1 tablespoon Dickey's Rib Rub or Dickey's Chili Pork Butt Rub

½ cup Dickey's Original Barbecue Sauce

32 ounces beef broth

1 tablespoon Worcestershire sauce

2 teaspoons sea salt

½ teaspoon freshly ground black pepper

6 crisp hoagie buns, split

6 tablespoons mayonnaise

6 slices provolone cheese

DIRECTIONS Preheat a smoker or grill to 250 degrees for non-caramelized onions or to 275 degrees for caramelized onions. Place the butter in a foil roasting pan on the rack of the smoker. Smoke until the butter is melted. Spread the onions and garlic in the pan. Smoke for 90 minutes or until the onions are light brown, stirring every 20 minutes and opening and closing the lid quickly to keep in as much heat as possible. Add the Dickey's Rib Rub and Dickey's Original Barbecue Sauce. Smoke until the onions are medium brown. Combine the broth and Worcestershire sauce in a separate foil pan. Smoke for 20 minutes or until the broth mixture is heated. Add the salt and pepper. Reheat the brisket for 5 to 6 minutes in the broth if needed; do not boil the meat.

Preheat the oven to 400 degrees. Bake the buns until toasted. Maintain the oven temperature. Spread 1 tablespoon of the mayonnaise over the bottom half of each hoagie roll. Add a generous portion of the brisket to the bottom buns. Divide the smoked onions evenly over the top of the brisket. Cut the provolone cheese into halves and place over the onions. Bake for 1 minute or just until the cheese is melted; do not overbake. Place the top bun over the cheese and serve with the heated smoky au jus.

> *Making the Smoked Brisket Dip Sandwich is extremely easy. This is a great recipe to use when reheating leftover brisket from the previous day's meal or leftover brisket from the restaurant."*

BRISKET-STUFFED
BURGERS

Prep Time: 1 hour **Difficulty:** Medium **Serves:** 4

INGREDIENTS

8 ounces smoked brisket, chopped

1 cup shredded mild Cheddar cheese

1¼ pounds 80/20 ground beef

4 teaspoons Dickey's Beef Brisket Rub

4 slices Cheddar cheese

2 tablespoons unsalted butter, melted

4 brioche buns, split

4 tablespoons mayonnaise

Leaf lettuce, beefsteak tomato, red onion slices, and pickles, for serving

DIRECTIONS

Combine the brisket and shredded Cheddar cheese in a bowl and mix well. Divide the ground beef into 4 equal portions and shape each portion into a ball. Shape a pocket in each ball and stuff each pocket with equal portions of the brisket mixture. Reshape the ball around the stuffing, packing tightly. Shape into 1-inch patties, keeping the filling in the center. Season each patty with 1 teaspoon of the Dickey's Beef Brisket Rub, seasoning all sides. Arrange on a plate and place in a cooler. Let stand for 30 to 40 minutes. Preheat the smoker to 275 degrees or until smoke is running thin, using Dickey's Oak Pellets for a stick smoker or Dickey's Competition Pellet blend for a pellet smoker. Arrange the burgers in the smoker. Smoke undisturbed for 20 minutes. Top each patty with a slice of Cheddar cheese. Smoke for 5 minutes. Remove to a plate and let rest for 5 minutes. Preheat a griddle and brush with the butter. Toast the buns in the butter. Remove the bottom buns to a plate. Spread each with 1 tablespoon of the mayonnaise. Add the patties, lettuce, tomato, onion, pickles, and top bun.

HONEYMOON AT LOTTA BURGER

Mr. and Mrs. Roland Dickey, Sr., were married in Albuquerque, New Mexico. With the family restaurant in full swing back in Dallas, Texas, the newlyweds didn't have much time to honeymoon. They had their first dinner together as man and wife at a carhop joint called Lotta Burger. By this point, it was clear that the young couple would be restauranteurs, just like Roland's father. However, it was burgers, not barbecue, that piqued their interest. Maurine decided that if they were to embark on their own venture, she had better do the research. She went to work for a burger restaurant back in Texas and did everything from fry cook to running the cash register, eventually opening a restaurant called Country Burger. In just a few weeks, Roland and Maurine decided it was better to run the family barbecue restaurant rather than a burger concept. Now, decades later, the Dickey Family of Restaurants has launched three additional concepts, including Big Deal Burger. First developed as a virtual restaurant with digital ordering and delivery only, it's now rolling out as a stand-alone concept. Perhaps it was fate, after their honeymoon dinner, that brought the Dickeys back to selling burgers.

Maurine and Roland Dickey

Joanna Windham's
GRILLED SMOKED
MEAT LOAF

HOME OFFICE
GREATS

Prep Time: 3½ to 4½ hours (plus overnight)   **Difficulty:** Medium   **Serves:** 6 or 7

INGREDIENTS

2 pounds ground chuck

1 pound ground pork

1 cup Red Chili Rub, (recipe, page 82) divided

½ cup finely chopped yellow onion

4 cloves garlic, minced

2 large eggs, beaten

½ cup bread crumbs

½ sleeve Ritz crackers, finely crushed

DIRECTIONS

Combine the ground chuck, ground pork, ⅞ of the Red Chili Rub, onion, garlic, eggs, bread crumbs, and crackers in a large bowl and mix well. Press to remove any air pockets and shape into a loaf. Place the loaf in a loaf pan. Tap the pan on the counter and press the loaf to remove any remaining air pockets. Place in the refrigerator.

Preheat a smoker to 225 degrees or an oven to 250 degrees. Place the loaf pan on the rack. Smoke or bake for 3 to 4 hours or until a meat thermometer inserted near the center registers 165 degrees, or may grill the meat loaf over indirect heat for 3 to 4 hours. Let stand to cool for 20 minutes. Chill overnight.

Preheat the grill to 400 degrees. Remove the loaf to a cutting board. Cut crosswise into 1¼- to 1½-inch slices. Arrange on a grill. Grill for 4 to 5 minutes per side or until a meat thermometer inserted near the center registers 165 degrees. Brush with the remaining Red Chili Rub. Remove to a plate. May be served as a sandwich on a toasted bun with fresh tomato slices, onion slices, and sliced pickles.

66 *This recipe may look like it doesn't have much to it, but the Red Chili Rub takes this main dish to a whole new level. Cooking it slow and letting it cool overnight will yield a meat loaf that will not fall apart when sliced. This is not your average meat loaf!"*

PORCUPINE
MEATBALLS

Prep Time: 70 to 80 minutes   **Difficulty:** Easy   **Serves:** 4 to 6

INGREDIENTS

½ cup uncooked long grain rice

1½ cups tap water, divided

¼ sweet onion, diced

1 teaspoon kosher salt

½ teaspoon celery salt

⅛ teaspoon freshly ground black pepper

⅛ teaspoon garlic powder

1 pound lean ground beef

2 tablespoons vegetable oil

1 (15-ounce) can tomato sauce

2 tablespoons brown sugar

2 tablespoons Worcestershire sauce

Rice, pasta, or mashed potatoes, for serving

DIRECTIONS

Combine the rice, ½ cup of the water, onion, salt, celery salt, pepper, and garlic powder in a large bowl. Add the ground beef and mix well. Shape into 1½ inch balls.

Heat the vegetable oil in a large heavy saucepan over medium-high heat. Add the meatballs. Cook on all sides until evenly browned. Drain the pan drippings.

Combine the tomato sauce, brown sugar, Worcestershire sauce, and remaining 1 cup water in a bowl and mix well. Pour over the meatballs. Simmer, covered, over low heat for 1 hour.

Serve over rice. May make the meatballs smaller and serve with wooden picks as an appetizer.

Pit Master Gary Kolm's
WYOMING
CHILI

Prep Time: 3 hours, 20 minutes   **Difficulty:** Easy   **Serves:** 6 to 8

INGREDIENTS

1 pound ground spicy Italian pork sausage

1 pound chili-grind ground beef

60 ounces chili hot beans, preferably Kuner's

4 pounds tomatoes, diced with juice

1 large white onion, diced

1 green bell pepper, seeded and diced

2 poblano peppers, seeded and diced

2 large jalapeño peppers, diced with seeds

1 to 2 cups water

Sour cream and shredded Cheddar cheese, for topping

DIRECTIONS

Brown the ground sausage and ground beef in a large skillet over medium-high heat, stirring to crumble; drain. Combine the beans, tomatoes, onion, bell pepper, poblano peppers, and jalapeños in a large stockpot. Add the sausage mixture and mix well. Bring to a boil over medium heat. Add enough of the water to make of the desired consistency. Reduce the heat to low. Simmer, covered, for 3 hours, stirring occasionally. Ladle into soup bowls. Top with sour cream and Cheddar cheese.

> *Here is one of my favorites for Sunday afternoon football.*"

Pit Master Rene Bassett's
HOMEMADE
CHILI CON CARNE

Prep Time: 2 hours   **Difficulty:** Easy   **Serves:** 8 to 10

INGREDIENTS

3 pounds ground beef

1 medium onion, diced

4 tablespoons butter

1 teaspoon garlic powder

½ teaspoon curry powder

1 teaspoon sugar

½ cup soy sauce

1 cup golden raisins

4 (16-ounce) cans red kidney beans

19 ounces water

4 medium fresh tomatoes, cut into quarters

Hot cooked rice, for serving

Tabasco sauce (optional)

DIRECTIONS

Brown the ground beef in a 5-quart stockpot over medium-high heat, stirring to crumble. Drain, reserving the drippings in a bowl in the refrigerator. Sauté the onion in the butter in a skillet. Add to the ground beef. Stir in the garlic powder, curry powder, sugar, and soy sauce. Add the raisins and mix well. Add the kidney beans, filling each can a fourth full with water and adding the drippings to the chili. Stir in the tomatoes. Bring to a boil. Boil for 20 minutes. Simmer, covered, for 1½ hours or until thickened like gravy. Remove the fat from the top of the reserved drippings and add the drippings to the chili. Cook until heated through. Ladle over rice on plates and mix in a few dashes of Tabasco sauce.

66 *This recipe is very flavorful and has been passed down from my family. You can make it as spicy as your palate likes by increasing the Tabasco sauce."*

Betsy Orton's
SMOKED
LAMB SHANK

Prep Time: 7½ to 8 hours (plus overnight)   **Difficulty:** Medium   **Serves:** 4 to 6

INGREDIENTS

4 (1½-pound) lamb shanks

1½ cups Red Chili Rub (recipe, page 82), divided

4 tablespoons unsalted butter

Sweet Chili Pickled Red Onions (recipe, page 84), for serving

Rice and fresh tomato salad, for serving

DIRECTIONS

Pierce each lamb shank with a metal skewer or sharp knife 20 to 25 times to allow the marinade to penetrate the silver skin. Combine the lamb and 1 cup of the Red Chili Rub in a large bowl; cover. Marinate in the refrigerator overnight.

Prepare a smoker or grill with an offset fire using oak or pecan wood. Heat to 225 degrees. Smoke the lamb for 3 hours, turning every hour. Remove to a plate and brush with the remaining ½ cup Red Chili Rub.

Place each lamb shank on a piece of foil. Top with 1 tablespoon of the butter and wrap tightly with the foil. Smoke or bake at 225 degrees for 3 to 4 hours or until the lamb is tender. Let stand to rest in the foil for 30 minutes. Serve with Sweet Chili Pickled Red Onions, rice, and tomato salad. May use pulled lamb for tacos and add sliced cucumbers, ranch salad dressing, and Sweet Chili Pickled Red Onions.

66 *Smoked lamb is one of our favorites and is super impressive when you have company over. This recipe is wonderful when you are looking to try something new and pairs perfectly with a great cabernet or zinfandel.*"

Laura Rea Dickey's
FRIED
PORK CHOPS

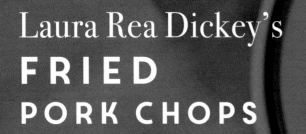

Prep Time: 25 to 30 minutes   **Difficulty:** Easy   **Serves:** 8

INGREDIENTS

8 bone-in pork chops

½ cup all-purpose flour

1 teaspoon seasoned salt

1 teaspoon black pepper

1 teaspoon Montreal steak seasoning

½ cup canola oil

1 tablespoon butter

DIRECTIONS

Rinse the pork chops and pat dry with paper towels, removing all excess moisture. Combine the flour, seasoned salt, pepper, and steak seasoning in a medium bowl and mix well. Dip both sides of the pork chops into the mixture and arrange on a plate.

Heat the canola oil to 350 degrees in a large skillet over medium-high heat. Add the butter and cook until melted. Add half the pork chops. Cook for 2 to 3 minutes or until golden brown. Turn the pork chops over. Cook for 1 to 2 minutes or until golden brown. Remove to a plate. Repeat the procedure with the remaining pork chops.

CITY

OF

LONDON

❝ *I love pairing this with a great pinot noir from Willamette Valley.*"

CATERING MAKES
ALL THE DIFFERENCE

In 1970, the Dickey's location in Richardson, Texas, wasn't doing very well. It didn't have the lunchtime crowd that the other restaurants enjoyed, and it was catering that saved it. With six or seven bobtail trucks, some warming boxes, some coolers, and a loading dock, they were able to serve Dickey's Barbecue to larger and larger crowds. In 1975, Ronald Reagan came to town to raise money for his second presidential run. Roland Dickey, Sr., had been around quite a few famous people before, but his impression of Ronald Reagan was similar to when he was introduced to John Wayne. He seemed larger than life and was one of the most charismatic people Dickey had ever met. The event was held on a ranch located in what is now Irving, Texas. At the time, it was one of Dickey's largest and most prestigious caterings.

Then in 1992, Ross Perot made his bid for the presidency, running against George H. W. Bush and Bill Clinton. Ross Perot was a longtime customer of Dickey's. During his campaign, Morley Safer of *60 Minutes* wanted to interview a few of Ross's friends in Dallas, and Ross mentioned Roland Dickey, Sr., to the producers. Morley Safer wanted to know what kind of man Ross was, and Roland let him know that Ross Perot was one of the kindest, most generous, and most honest men he'd ever known. Most of what he did for the city of Dallas went unrecognized.

After the first Gulf War in 1991, Dickey's fed 10,000 troops after a Saturday parade, and Mr. Perot paid for it. They didn't have a contract or a down payment. He simply said, "You feed the troops, and I'll pay you." That following week, his comptroller showed up at Dickey's catering headquarters and wrote them a check.

Another famous catering that comes to mind is when Burt Reynolds and his entourage filmed in North Texas for *Necessary Roughness*. Burt's signature laugh was genuine as Roland Dickey, Jr., met him in the original restaurant, where the cast and crew would often come in for dinner after filming. A signed picture from those days is still displayed in Central Bar. Most recently, Dickey's catered to barbecue lover and 2021 Academy of Country Music Awards' Video of the Year winner, Kane Brown.

Dickey's Barbecue Restaurants, Inc., has also served their Legit Texas Barbecue to folks at the Cattle Baron's Ball, the State Fair of Texas, and the Byron Nelson Golf Tournament. Today, all of their restaurants offer catering. Dickey's established 866-Barbecue as a direct line to our catering experts, so gatherings of any size can be planned, prepared, and delivered easily to guests nearest Dickey's restaurants.

Jermaine Martin's
PHO-INSPIRED
KETO BOWLS

HOME OFFICE GREATS

Prep Time: 25 to 30 minutes   **Difficulty:** Easy   **Serves:** 4

INGREDIENTS

32 ounces chicken broth

32 ounces vegetable broth

2 tablespoons chicken bone broth concentrate

1 tablespoon rice vinegar

1 teaspoon sesame oil

1 tablespoon liquid aminos

1 large head bok choy

1 teaspoon dried rosemary

1 teaspoon dried thyme

½ teaspoon ground allspice

½ teaspoon ground cinnamon

Salt to taste

4 cups frozen zucchini or squash noodles

1½ cups chopped green onions

½ small onion, thinly sliced

8 ounces cooked pork belly, thinly sliced

DIRECTIONS

Combine the chicken broth, vegetable broth, chicken bone broth concentrate, rice vinegar, sesame oil, and liquid aminos in a large stockpot. Bring to a boil.

Cut the leaves off the heart of the bok choy, reserving the leaves. Add the bok choy heart to the broth mixture. Add the rosemary, thyme, allspice, and cinnamon. Boil the broth mixture for 20 minutes. Season with salt. Remove and discard the bok choy heart. Remove the zucchini noodles from the freezer to thaw slightly. Chop the reserved bok choy leaves coarsely. Divide the zucchini noodles, bok choy leaves, green onions, onion, and pork belly among four bowls. Ladle the broth mixture over the top and serve.

 I like this meal because it's very filling and keto. It's also great on a cool day, sitting around the table and eating with family. You know you made it right when everyone is drinking from the bowl and asking for seconds."

SERRANO PINEAPPLE PIT HAM

Prep Time: 4 hours, 20 minutes   **Difficulty:** Medium   **Serves:** 10 to 15

INGREDIENTS

1 (13-pound) bone-in or boneless cured ham

2 (6-ounce) cans pineapple juice

1 serrano pepper, seeded

3 whole cloves

½ teaspoon ground black pepper

1 cup yellow mustard

1 pound light brown sugar

DIRECTIONS

Trim one end of the ham to create a base if using boneless ham. Cut the surface of the ham ¼ inch deep in a diamond pattern with a fillet knife if using unsliced ham.

Preheat the smoker to 225 degrees using apple or oak wood or any fruitwood.

Combine the pineapple juice, serrano pepper, cloves, and black pepper in a blender and process until the cloves are finely chopped. Place the flat end of the ham on a large piece of foil and fold up the edges to make a boat or use a foil pan. Rub the mustard over the ham and pack half the brown sugar over the mustard. Smoke the ham for 2 hours. Baste with a third of the pineapple juice mixture. Smoke for 1½ hours, basting with the pineapple juice mixture and drippings every 30 minutes. Baste the ham and pack with the remaining brown sugar. Smoke for 30 minutes or until a meat thermometer inserted in the thickest portion registers 145 degrees. Remove the ham to a platter. Let stand, uncovered, for 20 to 25 minutes.

NOTE

Even though this has a good coating of brown sugar and mustard on the outside, smoking this ham on the pit with the serrano pineapple basting liquid adds a kick of unforgettable flavor.

PIT HAM & CHEESE SLIDERS

Prep Time: 25 minutes   **Difficulty:** Easy   **Serves:** 6 to 12

INGREDIENTS

1 (12-pack) Hawaiian rolls

2 tablespoons cold unsalted butter

3 tablespoons mayonnaise (not sweet)

2 tablespoons yellow mustard

24 pickle chips of choice

16 ounces sliced Serrano Pineapple Pit Ham (recipe, page 164) or smoked ham

1½ cups shredded Cheddar cheese

DIRECTIONS

Preheat the oven or grill to 350 degrees. Cut the rolls as a whole crosswise into two layers. Cut a piece of foil large enough to enclose the rolls. Rub the butter thinly over one side of the foil. Place the bottom layer of the rolls cut side up on the foil. Spread the mayonnaise evenly over the cut side of the bottom layer of rolls. Spread the mustard over the cut side of the top layer and add 2 pickle chips in the center of each roll. Arrange the ham evenly over the bottom layer of the rolls and sprinkle with the cheese. Place the top layer cut side down over the bottom layer. Fold the foil over the rolls, sealing the front edge and sides tightly. Bake for 20 minutes. Cut into 12 sliders.

NOTE

The beauty of this foil-pack recipe is that you can utilize leftover holiday ham for a satisfying snack at home, on the patio, or even at the campsite. May premake the sandwiches and place in the refrigerator. Place in the oven or close to your campfire to heat until warm, cheesy, and delicious. The butter rubbed on the foil helps toast the top and bottom of the buns and adds a little crunch to the bite.

Mr. Dickey's
GRILLED CHEESE
SANDWICH

FAMILY FAVORITE

Prep Time: 5 minutes   **Difficulty:** Easy   **Serves:** 1

INGREDIENTS

1 tablespoon (about) unsalted butter

2 slices good-quality rustic bread

4 slices Cheddar cheese or Velveeta cheese

2 tablespoons real mayonnaise

DIRECTIONS

Spread a thin layer of butter on one side of each slice of bread. Place the Cheddar cheese on the buttered side of one slice of bread. Place the second slice of bread buttered side down on the cheese. Divide the mayonnaise and spread on both sides of the sandwich.

Melt the remaining butter in a skillet over medium heat. Cook the sandwich in the butter until crisp and the cheese is melted, turning once.

> *Grilled Cheese Sandwich. Americans suffer from having bread that's not very good. The first thing you need for a sandwich is some good bread. I go to a certain couple of places here in Dallas, where they've got really good bread, but I grew up eating the regular grocery store bread that everybody knows. That's the key that most Americans don't know."*

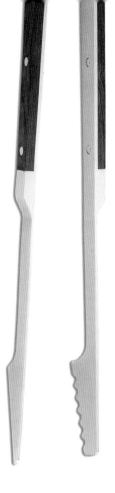

BARBECUE
SAUSAGES

Can you just throw some sausage on the grill and hope for the best?

Sure. But understanding what makes a good sausage great on the grill or barbecue is part of being a backyard Pit Master. Here are some different types of sausages that you can cook on the grill and some unique techniques.

ALREADY-COOKED SAUSAGE

This could be anything from a Polish kielbasa or andouille to any smoked sausage at the grocery store. The goal is to keep the casing from drying out. Pruning or overheating the casing will cause the sausage to render out too much fat. Here are some simple pointers:

- **Heat Source**

  Heat the grill or pit to 250 to 275 degrees and make sure the fire is offset (meaning off to one side and not under the meat). On a pellet grill, place the sausages on an elevated rack. I always prefer using a hardwood like oak or hickory for this process. Fruitwoods are acceptable options, too.

- **Time and Temperature**

  Most 1-pound sausages will heat to 145 degrees within 17 to 22 minutes at these temperatures. Most importantly, take the temperature through the end of the sausage; do not pierce the casing on the sides because moisture will pour out and reduce the quality of the sausage.

- **Color, Texture, and Taste**

  This process will slightly darken the casing of the sausage and slightly dry it out, yielding a sausage with a "snap" when you slice and bite into it. It will add a little deeper smoke flavor, but the interior of the sausage will retain all the original flavor and moisture. Always slice your sausage on a bias; we do not want to serve pepperoni slices!

RAW SAUSAGE, FULLY COOKED ON THE GRILL

Now, we are talking about most sausages at the butcher case or packaged-meat area in the grocery store. These could be Italian sausage, chicken sausage, or any unique flavor of grilling sausage. The number one goal is to fully cook the sausage so it is safe to eat, so having a thermometer is important. The second goal is to manage the heat and movement of the sausage so that it does not split too early in the grilling process. Here are the basics:

- **Heat Source**

  Heat the grill or pit to 350 degrees and make sure your charcoal or wood has burned for a time so that the heat is even and controlled. On a pellet grill, just set the temperature to 350 degrees. Here, wood selection is important as it imparts a lot of flavor to the sausage. Fruitwoods and flavorful woods like mesquite work very well.

- **Time and Temperature**

  Most 4- to 5-ounce sausages will heat to 165 degrees within 12 to 15 minutes at these temperatures. Most importantly, take the temperature through the end of the sausage; do not pierce the casing on the sides because moisture will pour out and reduce the quality of the sausage.

- **Color, Texture, and Taste**

  When I start cooking sausages on the grill, I place them on the outside perimeter of the grill. This way the heat and smoke are kissing the sides of the sausages. Cover the grill with the lid and make sure the vents are open. I carefully flip the sausages every 2 minutes so they cook evenly and do not burn. If you like to have a little char on the outside of the sausages, you can move them to the center of the grill during the last 4 to 5 minutes, and let them grill, flipping every minute. Move sausages away from any flare-ups; burning grease will give them a gasoline flavor—not good!

RAW SAUSAGE, COOKED IN A FLAVORED BATH AND THEN GRILLED

Now, we are talking about sausages like brats but could also include Italian sausages and uniquely flavored sausages. The number one goal is to add flavor to the sausages while fully cooking them so they are safe to eat. Having a thermometer is important. The second goal is to enhance the flavor you just added with some good hot grilling. Here are some tips:

- **Flavor Bath**

  Cooking sausage in a flavor bath imparts flavor just below the surface of the casing; however, it does not travel deep into the sausage, so using good-quality ingredients ensures maximum flavor. Making beer brats is all about a good amber beer that is not too hoppy but has body. Also, don't forget the onions, caraway seeds, black peppercorns, and a bay leaf. Italian sausage or garlic sausage can be simmered in a broth of dry white wine, onions, garlic, fennel seeds, black peppercorns, and a bay leaf. For all flavor baths, heat all of the ingredients except the sausage over medium-high heat in a saucepan and simmer for 5 minutes to get all the flavors to release. Add the sausage and simmer the liquid so that the sausage heats slowly and does not split. Heat the sausage to 160 degrees as it will continue to cook when you take it out of the bath and grill it. A 4- to 5-ounce sausage should take 10 to 12 minutes to fully cook.

- **Flavor Meet Grill**

  Heat the grill to 350 to 400 degrees. The goal here is to add a little char to the outside of the sausage. It will not be on the grill for more than 5 to 8 minutes, so if it splits a little, you will not lose much juice from the sausage. Keep the sausage moving every minute, keeping the top on the grill to capture the smoke to add a little flavor.

- **Color, Texture, and Taste**

  The skin of the sausage should pick up grill marks and a little charring. The texture of the skin should be slightly crisp as the high-heat grilling dries it out slightly. Three flavors are present: the high-heat grilling flavor on the outside of the skin, the flavor bath ingredients trapped just below the casing, and finally the sausage itself and all of its ingredients.

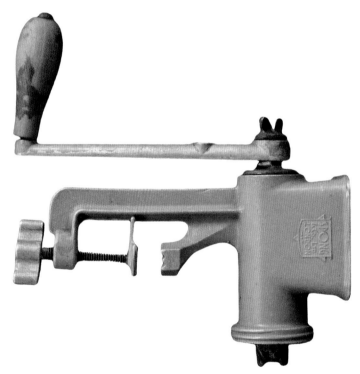

Roland Dickey, Jr.'s
SPICY JALAPEÑO
CHEDDAR SAUSAGE

Prep Time: 22 minutes　　　**Difficulty:** Easy　　　**Serves:** 2 to 3

INGREDIENTS　　　1 (12-ounce) Dickey's Jalapeño Cheddar Sausage

DIRECTIONS　　　Preheat a smoker or grill with an offset coal bed to 250 to 275 degrees. Place the sausage over indirect heat. Smoke, covered, with the vents open for 14 to 16 minutes or until a meat thermometer inserted in one end registers 145 degrees and the skin of the sausage is dark and crisp; do not overheat or cook too quickly. Remove to a cutting board. Let stand, uncovered, to rest for 4 to 5 minutes. Cut diagonally into ¼-inch slices.

NOTE　　　*After nearly sixty years since opening in 1941, we set out to provide folks the most flavorful sausage, packed with as much Cheddar and jalapeños as humanly possible. This sausage begins with our popular Polish-style sausage, infuses it with massive volumes of Cheddar cheese, and fires it up with jalapeños, cracked black pepper, and old-world spices. Once we perfected the recipe, I knew we had to go full force with the best-tasting sausage you could possibly get.*

❝ *Cheese and spice makes everything better!"*

EVOLUTION OF DICKEY'S CULT FOLLOWING FOR KIELBASA SAUSAGE

Dickey's sausages are unique and specially curated for our restaurants. Roland Dickey, Sr., introduced the original Dickey's Kielbasa Sausage in the 80s, which was made available to grocery stores because of its popularity. In 2010, Roland Dickey, Jr., took the kielbasa sausage recipe to the next level by adding jalapeños and cheese. Both types of kielbasa sausage sell out often. Dickey's Kielbasa is a U-shaped smoked sausage made from pork. The meat is cured, ground with fat, enriched with secret spices, and then packed into a nitrate- and nitrite-free casing.

Guests continued to ask for different varieties of sausages. Chef Phil, Roland Dickey, Jr., Laura Rea, and Nick Schwabe jumped on the opportunity to start developing and producing small-batch craft sausages in specialty varieties. Dickey's Craft Sausage Company was created, where each sausage rope is hand prepared, curated, and packed. Dickey's Craft Sausage Company develops and produces over twenty types of gourmet, chef-curated sausages that are currently sold online through the Barbecue at Home website. Brisket Pastrami Sausages, French Onion Soup Sausages, Brisket Burnt Ends Sausages, Habanero Jerk Chicken Sausages, and Broccoli Cheddar Chicken Sausages are just a few of the most popular small-batch varieties. On barbecueathome.com, you can build your own sausage box and choose from Dickey's small-batch, craft sausages made from the freshest premium beef, chicken, and pork to smoke, grill, or roast in your favorite skillet.

Maja Perušić's
TAVCHE GRAVCHE

HOME OFFICE GREATS

Prep Time: 1¾ to 2¾ hours   **Difficulty:** Easy   **Serves:** 4 to 6

INGREDIENTS

3 tablespoons olive oil

2 pounds onions, cut into ¼-inch pieces

1 pound well-drained canned navy beans (1 or 2 cans)

½ cup tomato purée

2 tablespoons paprika

1 tablespoon garlic powder

1 teaspoon kosher salt

½ teaspoon freshly ground black pepper

1 teaspoon chili powder

⅛ teaspoon cayenne pepper, or to taste

4 medium-spice Italian sausages

1 tablespoon chopped fresh parsley

> *This is traditionally made with a Macedonian-style sausage that is made with a good amount of leeks and spices, but a medium-spice Italian sausage would be a good substitute. Even Dickey's Smoked Polish Sausage would work."*

DIRECTIONS   Heat the olive oil in a large saucepan over medium heat. Cook the onions in the oil until very tender, stirring frequently. Remove half the onions to a plate and reserve. Add the beans and tomato purée to the onions in the saucepan. Add enough water to cover the mixture. Stir in the paprika, garlic powder, salt, black pepper, chili powder, and cayenne pepper. Cook, covered, for 1 or 2 hours, stirring occasionally and adding additional water if the mixture is too dry.

Preheat the broiler to high 15 minutes before the beans are done. Line a baking pan with foil. Split the sausages into halves with a sharp knife and arrange casing sides down on the prepared baking pan. Press the sausages lightly to flatten slightly. Broil on the second oven rack for 5 to 6 minutes. Set the oven to 475 degrees.

Spoon the bean mixture into a baking dish, Dutch oven, or large clay pot. Arrange the reserved onions over the bean mixture. Sprinkle with the parsley and top with the browned sausages. Bake, uncovered, until a crust forms over the top of the beans and sausage.

Pit Master Darryl Weaver's
BEER BRATS

Prep Time: 20 to 30 minutes   **Difficulty:** Easy   **Serves:** 10

INGREDIENTS

10 brats

4 cans lager beer

1 yellow onion, sliced

2 teaspoons red pepper flakes

1 teaspoon garlic powder

½ teaspoon black pepper

1 teaspoon salt

DIRECTIONS

Combine the brats, beer, onion, red pepper flakes, garlic powder, black pepper, and salt in a large deep skillet over medium-high heat. Bring to a boil. Boil for 10 minutes or until the brats turn white. Remove the brats to a plate. Drain the onion and reserve.

Preheat the grill to at least 375 degrees. Grill the brats over direct heat for 2 to 3 minutes, turning twice with tongs to ensure casings are crisp and slightly split. Serve with the onion on the side or serve in soft brat or sausage buns. May steam the buns on a wire rack placed over the beer mixture.

NOTE

I recommend getting your brats from a local meat market.

" *I enjoy grilling out with friends and family during the summer. At one of our gatherings, my buddies decided to have a cook-off, and this recipe for beer brats was the final winner.*"

SMOKED BOLOGNA
SANDWICH

Prep Time: 3 to 4 hours   **Difficulty:** Medium   **Serves:** 10 to 12

INGREDIENTS

1 (4- to 5-pound) stick bologna

½ cup yellow mustard

½ cup Chili Pork Rub (recipe, page 78)

2 beefsteak tomatoes, cut into ¼-inch slices

1 yellow onion

1 head iceberg lettuce

¾ to 1 cup yellow mustard

1 loaf Texas-style white bread, sliced and toasted

¾ to 1 cup mayonnaise

DIRECTIONS

Preheat the smoker to 250 degrees using Dickey's Oak or Hickory Pellets. Score the surface of the bologna ¼ to ½ inch deep in a 1-inch crisscross pattern using a fillet knife. Rub ½ cup mustard over the bologna. Season evenly with the Chili Pork Rub. Place the bologna on the rack of the smoker. Smoke for 3 to 4 hours or until darkened. Let stand at room temperature until the exterior is cooled and slightly dry. Cut into ½-inch slices.

Cut the tomatoes into ¼-inch slices. Cut the onion into ¼-inch slices and separate into rings. Remove the core of the lettuce and cut the head into fourths.

Spread 1 heaping tablespoon of mustard on one piece of toast and top with a slice of bologna. Layer with a lettuce leaf, tomato slice, and a few onion rings. Top with a second piece of toast spread with 1 heaping tablespoon of the mayonnaise. Repeat the procedure with the remaining ingredients.

NOTE

It's true—we've improved upon the quintessential American sandwich. Season a whole bologna stick using the Chili Pork Rub (recipe, page 78) and then smoke using Dickey's Oak or Hickory Pellets. Put a ½-inch slice on Texas Toast, add your accoutrements of choice, and chow down!

Pit Master Tom Eggerud's
BRUNSWICK
STEW

Prep Time: 1½ hours   **Difficulty:** Easy   **Serves:** 10 to 12

INGREDIENTS

½ cup unsalted butter

2 yellow onions, chopped

3 cloves garlic, minced

4 cups chicken stock

2 (8-ounce) cans
tomato sauce

1 (28-ounce) can
crushed tomatoes

1 (16-ounce) package frozen
lima beans

1 (16-ounce) package frozen
corn or fresh corn

2 cups Dickey's Original
Barbecue Sauce

1 pound pulled pork

1½ pounds smoked chicken,
pulled or chopped

Salt and black
pepper to taste

Saltines or warm corn bread,
for serving

DIRECTIONS

Heat the smoker or grill to 350 degrees. Melt the butter in a large heavy pot in the smoker. Add the onions and garlic. Cook for 8 to 10 minutes or until translucent, stirring frequently; do not brown. Add the chicken stock, tomato sauce, crushed tomatoes, lima beans, corn, Dickey's Original Barbecue Sauce, pork, and chicken. Simmer with the cover closed for 1 hour, stirring every 10 minutes. Season with salt and pepper if needed. Ladle into soup bowls and serve with saltines or corn bread.

 Brunswick Stew is a great way to use leftover smoked pork butt and chicken. I even make a version of this with leftover smoked turkey after Thanksgiving. Better than a leftover turkey and stuffing sandwich!"

WIFE'S POLITICAL CAREER ENDS HUSBAND'S COOKING SHOW

In 2004, after many years serving Texas in the nonprofit sector, I decided to run for County Commissioner in Dallas's District 1. Previously, I had headed up the child welfare program for the State of Texas, and I also served as chairwoman of Parkland Health and Hospital System's Board of Visitors. With these valuable experiences, I knew I was ready for public office. It just so happened that when I announced my candidacy, Roland was doing a weekly cooking show on WFAA's *Good Morning Texas*. The ABC-affiliate executives made the decision to cancel his segment in a preemptive attempt to avoid showing favoritism to the Dickey family.

Roland's segments came on in the morning and news coverage of my spirited campaign was playing on the nightly news. Soon after, the *Dallas Morning News* ran an article entitled "Wife's Political Career Ends Husband's Cooking Show." Don't you feel sorry for Roland! Things always seem to work out for him. A few days after the article ran, a country radio station, 99.5 The Wolf, called to ask if he'd move his cooking show over to their station. They thought it was hilarious that my political ambitions abruptly canceled his television appearances. Roland and The Wolf went on for a couple of years after that, broadcasting weekly cooking tips, recipes, and anecdotes.

Roland Dickey doing a radio program for 99.5 The Wolf

Simone Dominguez's
CHICKEN
ENCHILADA SOUP

Prep Time: 20 to 30 minutes   **Difficulty:** Easy   **Serves:** 6 to 8

INGREDIENTS

2 tablespoons avocado oil

1 small white onion, diced

2 cloves garlic, minced

½ cup masa harina

3 cups chicken stock

2 cups shredded rotisserie or smoked chicken

1¼ cups (10 ounces) enchilada sauce

1 (15-ounce) can black beans, rinsed and drained

1 (15-ounce) can fire-roasted diced tomatoes

1 (4-ounce) can chopped green Hatch peppers

1 teaspoon salt

½ teaspoon ground cumin

8 ounces sharp Cheddar cheese, grated

Tortilla chips or strips, diced avocados, shredded sharp Cheddar cheese, sour cream, chopped fresh cilantro, and/or pico de gallo, for topping

DIRECTIONS

Heat the avocado oil in a large stockpot over medium-high heat. Add the onion. Sauté for 5 minutes or until translucent. Add the garlic. Sauté for 1 minute or until fragrant. Stir in the masa harina. Cook for 1 minute. Add half the chicken stock and stir until well mixed. Add the remaining chicken stock and stir until well mixed. Add the chicken, enchilada sauce, black beans, undrained tomatoes, Hatch peppers, salt, and cumin and stir to mix. Bring to a simmer, stirring occasionally. Reduce the heat to medium-low. Simmer for 3 minutes, stirring occasionally to prevent sticking. Stir in the 8 ounces Cheddar cheese a handful at a time. Adjust the salt. Ladle into soup bowls and top with tortilla chips, avocados, Cheddar cheese, sour cream, cilantro, and/or pico de gallo.

66 *This is the perfect soup to cook in the winter months. It's a staple in our home, and we hope you enjoy!"*

Mrs. Dickey's
HERBED CHICKEN & VEGETABLE SHEET PAN DINNER

FAMILY FAVORITE

Prep Time: 35 to 45 minutes **Difficulty:** Easy **Serves:** 6 to 8

INGREDIENTS

Olive oil, for greasing

2 pounds chicken breasts, cut into 1-inch strips

1½ cups petite baby carrots

1 (14-ounce) can chickpeas, drained and rinsed

1 pound baby red potatoes, cut into halves

3 tablespoons olive oil, divided

1 teaspoon dried basil

1 teaspoon dried thyme

1 teaspoon dried oregano

1 teaspoon paprika

½ teaspoon garlic powder

Mineral salt and freshly cracked pepper to taste

1 pound asparagus, trimmed and cut into thirds

½ large yellow onion, sliced

Chopped fresh parsley to taste

1 avocado, sliced, for serving

DIRECTIONS

Preheat the oven to 425 degrees. Line a rimmed baking sheet with foil and grease lightly with olive oil. Arrange the chicken, carrots, and chickpeas on the prepared baking sheet. Add the potatoes skins sides up. Drizzle with 1½ tablespoons of the olive oil.

Combine the basil, thyme, oregano, paprika, garlic powder, salt, and pepper in a small bowl and mix well. Sprinkle ¾ of the basil mixture evenly over the chicken and vegetables and toss to coat. Roast for 20 to 25 minutes.

Push the chicken mixture to one side of the baking sheet. Arrange the asparagus and onion on the baking sheet and drizzle with the remaining 1½ tablespoons olive oil. Sprinkle with the remaining basil mixture and toss to coat. Roast for 10 to 15 minutes. Let stand at room temperature to cool and steam for 5 minutes before serving. Divide the mixture evenly among 6 to 8 bowls. Sprinkle with parsley. Serve with avocado.

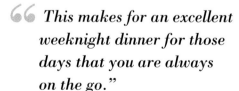

66 *This makes for an excellent weeknight dinner for those days that you are always on the go."*

WOMEN OF THE PIT

Barbecue is often pictured as a man standing over a smoker. There are certainly a lot of great men behind the grill. However, folks are intrigued to learn that at Dickey's, it's more likely to be a woman overseeing the pit. Dickey's Barbecue Restaurants, Inc., is a female-led company in many ways. Laura Rea Dickey, CEO of Dickey's Barbecue Restaurants, Inc., is not alone at the top. Dickey's has more C-level executives that are women than are men and more female team leaders, too.

Renee Roozen serves as CAO and has been with the company six years. Trinity Hall leads construction. Shayla Partusch leads purchasing. Carissa De Santis serves as CIO, leading technology. Kristin Peterson serves a CMO. Jamie Henretta serves as Creative Director. Lauren Lumbley leads communications. Tonya Pollock leads travel. Sara Kamal leads legal. The impressive list of leading ladies goes on and on. Dickey's also has many female franchise partners and has set up a mentoring program for women restaurant owners.

The Dickey Foundation also is led by two women: Founder and Chairwoman Maurine Dickey and Executive Director Betsy Orton. Dickey's is proud to celebrate the many talented females who lead the world's largest barbecue concept. "I'm proud to

work for a company that supports women's career advancement," Laura Rea Dickey said. "Men have long been key players in business and in barbecue, but women have shown we definitely have a seat at the table and a place at the barbecue pit. We focus on always finding the best person for the job, and we just make sure to not overlook leading ladies. Companies need different perspectives and talents to make their businesses stronger. Roland and I are very fortunate to have many incredible folks leading the Dickey's team. Ed Herman, our amazing EVP of Operations, Chef Phil Butler, CFO Jay Rooney, and SVP of Franchise Relations Jeff Gruber round out our executive leadership team. These folks truly make Dickey's exceptional."

LONE STAR®
BEER CAN CHICKEN

Prep Time: 2½ hours (plus 6 to 12 hours)   **Difficulty:** Medium   **Serves:** 2 to 4

INGREDIENTS

1 (4-pound) chicken

1 lemon, cut into quarters

1 lime, cut into quarters

5 tablespoons chopped garlic

4 tablespoons poultry seasoning

½ yellow onion, cut into 1-inch pieces

1 (12-ounce) can Lone Star Beer

2 cups The Spritz (recipe, page 81)

DIRECTIONS

Remove the parts from the cavity of the chicken. Pat the chicken dry with a paper towel. Tuck the wing tips behind the chicken, away from the breasts. Squeeze the lemon juice and lime juice over the entire surface and cavity of the chicken, reserving the lemon and lime. Rub all of the garlic in the cavity. Sprinkle half the poultry seasoning over the surface of the chicken and half in the cavity. Place the reserved lemon, reserved lime, and onion in the cavity. Place the chicken in a pan and cover with plastic wrap. Chill for 6 to 12 hours to marinate.

Preheat the grill to 275 degrees. Drink a fourth of the beer. Remove the plastic wrap from the chicken. Insert the beer can upright into the cavity of the chicken, keeping the onion, lemon, and lime in the cavity. Place the can upright in the center of the grill with the chicken standing up. Spray generously with The Spritz. Close the lid. Grill for 2 hours or until a meat thermometer inserted in a breast registers 160 to 165 degrees and inserted in a thigh registers 170 degrees, spraying generously with The Spritz every 30 minutes. Let stand on the can at room temperature for 10 minutes. Remove the beer can and place the chicken on a cutting board. Carve the chicken.

CHICKEN & BISCUIT
CASSEROLE

Prep Time: 45 minutes **Difficulty:** Medium **Serves:** 8

INGREDIENTS

6 tablespoons unsalted butter

1 yellow onion, chopped

½ cup chopped celery

½ cup chopped peeled carrots

½ cup all-purpose flour

3 cups chicken stock

1 teaspoon kosher salt

½ teaspoon ground black pepper

¼ teaspoon ground white pepper

1 cup heavy cream

8 ounces frozen green peas

8 ounces frozen corn kernels

1 smoked or rotisserie chicken, shredded

1 (8-count) can biscuits

½ cup shredded mild Cheddar cheese

DIRECTIONS

Preheat the oven to 350 degrees. Melt the butter in a large stockpot over medium-high heat. Add the onion, celery, and carrots. Cook for 3 to 4 minutes or until tender. Add the flour gradually, whisking constantly. Cook for 1 minute, whisking constantly.

Add the chicken stock gradually, whisking constantly to remove all lumps. Whisk in the salt, black pepper, and white pepper. Whisk in the cream. Bring just to a simmer over medium-low heat. Simmer until thickened. Adjust salt and pepper.

Add the green peas, corn, and chicken and stir to mix well. Spoon into a 9x13-inch baking dish. Arrange the biscuits evenly over the top. Sprinkle with the Cheddar cheese. Bake for 20 minutes or until the top is golden brown and the filling is hot and bubbly. Let stand to cool slightly before serving.

Gary's Grandma's
CHICKEN &
SPANISH CAULIFLOWER RICE

HOME OFFICE GREATS ★

Prep Time: 1 hour (plus 2 to 3 hours)　　**Difficulty:** Easy　　**Serves:** 4

INGREDIENTS

2 pounds boneless skinless chicken thighs

1 teaspoon chili powder

½ teaspoon garlic powder

2 teaspoons Himalayan sea salt

¾ teaspoon ground cumin

½ teaspoon freshly ground black pepper

2 tablespoons olive oil, divided

3 jalapeño peppers, seeded, stemmed, and cut into ¼-inch pieces

½ yellow onion, chopped

2 (28-ounce) cans diced tomatoes

1 (8-ounce) can tomato sauce

1 (16-ounce) package cauliflower pearls

DIRECTIONS

Place the chicken in a large bowl. Combine the chili powder, garlic powder, sea salt, cumin, and black pepper in a small bowl and mix well. Sprinkle over the chicken and toss to coat. Marinate in the refrigerator for 2 to 3 hours.

Heat 1 tablespoon of the olive oil in a medium saucepan over medium-high heat. Add the jalapeños and onion. Sauté until tender. Add the chicken, undrained tomatoes, and tomato sauce. Simmer over medium heat for 35 to 40 minutes or until the chicken is cooked through.

Heat the remaining 1 tablespoon olive oil in a saucepan over medium-high heat. Add the cauliflower pearls. Cook for 1 minute or until lightly toasted, stirring to coat. Stir in 2 or 3 ladles of the sauce. Cook, covered, over medium heat for 15 minutes. Divide the cauliflower rice among 4 plates. Top each with equal portions of the chicken and sauce.

> " *This recipe is bursting with flavor. Everyone at your dinner table will be asking for more!*"

Cullen Dickey's
30-MINUTE CREAMY
CHICKEN & BROCCOLI PASTA

FAMILY FAVORITE

Prep Time: 35 to 45 minutes   **Difficulty:** Medium   **Serves:** 4 to 6

INGREDIENTS

Salt to taste

8 ounces bowtie pasta

1 tablespoon olive oil

10 ounces broccoli, cut into 1-inch florets

¼ cup plus 3 tablespoons vegetable oil, divided

1 tablespoon dried Italian seasoning to taste

Pepper to taste

1½ pounds boneless skinless chicken breasts, diced or cut into strips

4 cloves garlic, minced

1 cup heavy cream

1¼ cups shredded mozzarella cheese

1 teaspoon dried chives to taste (optional)

½ cup milk

1 teaspoon chopped fresh curly parsley (optional)

2 tablespoons shredded Parmesan cheese to taste (optional)

DIRECTIONS

Bring a large pot of salted water to a boil over high heat. Add the pasta. Boil for 10 minutes or until al dente; drain. Toss with the olive oil.

Combine the broccoli, ¼ cup of the vegetable oil, Italian seasoning, salt, and pepper in a saucepan. Cook, covered, for 15 to 20 minutes or until cooked through, stirring occasionally.

Season the chicken liberally with salt and pepper. Brown the chicken in the remaining 3 tablespoons vegetable oil in a large skillet over medium-high heat. Cook for 10 minutes or until a meat thermometer inserted in the thickest portion registers 165 degrees. Remove to a plate, reserving the pan drippings.

Reduce the heat to medium. Add the garlic to the reserved pan drippings. Sauté for 30 seconds; do not burn. Add the heavy cream. Bring just to a simmer. Add the mozzarella cheese and chives. Cook until the cheese is melted and the mixture is creamy, stirring constantly. Reduce the heat to medium-low. Add the milk gradually, whisking constantly. Simmer until thickened and creamy. Add the pasta, chicken, and broccoli and toss to coat. Serve topped with parsley or Parmesan cheese.

“ *This satisfying, savory dish is famous because of its creamy mozzarella sauce. By slowly heating together cream, milk, olive oil, salt, pepper, and Italian seasoning and then finishing with chives, the chicken and broccoli are secondary to the sauce.*”

CHICKEN & RICE
AU GRATIN

Prep Time: 2 hours   **Difficulty:** Medium   **Serves:** 8 to 10

INGREDIENTS

1 chicken, cut into quarters

2 cups chicken stock

3 cups water

1 yellow onion, cut into quarters

3 ribs celery, cut into pieces

2 bay leaves

1 bunch broccoli

½ cup unsalted butter

8 ounces cremini mushrooms, sliced

¼ cup all-purpose flour

2 cups whole milk

1½ cups cooked white rice

Salt and pepper to taste

½ cup grated Parmesan cheese

DIRECTIONS

Combine the chicken, chicken stock, water, onion, celery, and bay leaves in a large stockpot. Bring to a simmer over medium-high heat. Cook, covered, over medium-low heat for 45 minutes or until the chicken can be pulled apart with a fork. Remove the chicken to a tray, reserving the broth. Let stand to cool for 20 minutes. Shred the chicken finely, discarding the skin and bones. Strain the broth and reserve 1 cup.

Cut the broccoli into bite-size florets. Place on a microwave-safe plate and cover with a damp paper towel. Microwave on high for 2 minutes.

Preheat the oven or grill to 375 degrees. Melt the butter in a saucepan over medium heat. Add the mushrooms. Cook for 5 minutes, stirring frequently. Stir in the flour. Cook for 1 minute, stirring occasionally. Add the milk and reserved broth gradually, stirring constantly. Bring to a boil. Reduce the heat to medium-low. Cook for 5 minutes or just until thickened, stirring constantly. Remove from the heat. Stir in the broccoli, rice, and chicken. Season with salt and pepper if needed. Spoon into a baking dish or 12-inch cast-iron skillet. Spread the Parmesan cheese evenly over the top. Bake or grill for 30 minutes or until hot and bubbly and the top is light brown.

Pit Master Karen Edwards'
FAMOUS
CHICKEN SALAD

Prep Time: 10 minutes   **Difficulty:** Easy   **Serves:** 4

INGREDIENTS

2 whole Dickey's smoked chicken breasts

1 small yellow onion, peeled

2 or 3 ribs celery with leaves

2 cups mayonnaise

1 tablespoon spicy mustard

½ teaspoon garlic powder

¼ teaspoon ground black pepper

Kosher salt to taste

DIRECTIONS

Shred the chicken by hand; do not use a knife. Process the onion and celery in a food processor until minced. Combine the chicken, onion mixture, mayonnaise, mustard, garlic powder, pepper, and salt in a large bowl and mix well. Chill for 2 hours or until serving time.

66 *It's always better if you can chill the salad for 2 hours before serving cold. Serve immediately for a hot pressed chicken sandwich with gouda cheese and bacon!"*

CAJUN
FRIED TURKEY

Prep Time: 1 hour (plus overnight)   **Difficulty:** High   **Serves:** 10 to 12

INGREDIENTS

2 cups salted butter

½ yellow onion

6 garlic cloves

¼ cup Worcestershire sauce

2 tablespoons ground black pepper

2 tablespoons (or more) Cajun seasoning

¼ cup Louisiana-style hot sauce

½ bottle cold domestic beer

1 (12- to 14-pound) turkey

Peanut or vegetable oil, for frying

DIRECTIONS

Microwave the butter in a microwave-safe bowl just until melted. Combine the butter, onion, garlic, Worcestershire sauce, pepper, 2 tablespoons Cajun seasoning, and hot sauce in a blender. Process on high speed for 1 minute or until the onion and garlic are liquefied. Add the beer through the hole in the lid, processing constantly. Pour the mixture through a mesh strainer.

Place the turkey in a large pan. Inject the marinade all over the turkey, including the legs, back, wings, thighs, and breasts. May sprinkle with an additional 2 tablespoons Cajun seasoning. Marinate, covered, in the refrigerator overnight.

Place the turkey on a hanger and lower the hanger into a large pot. Add enough peanut oil to cover the turkey by 1 inch. Transfer the turkey back to the pan. Heat the peanut oil over a large propane burner to 375 degrees. Lower the turkey on the hanger into the oil. Deep-fry, uncovered, for 3 minutes per pound or until a meat thermometer inserted in the thickest portion of the thigh registers 180 degrees and inserted in a breast registers 165 degrees. Remove the turkey and drain well. Place on a wire rack to rest until the skin is dry and crisp. May sprinkle with additional Cajun seasoning before marinating or after frying the turkey.

Roland Dickey, Jr.'s
EASY DUCK
CONFIT

Prep Time: 4 to 4¼ hours   **Difficulty:** Medium   **Serves:** 2

INGREDIENTS

2 duck legs

2 teaspoons sea salt

2 cups light olive oil or rendered duck fat

DIRECTIONS

Pat the duck legs dry with paper towels. Prick the skin all over with a needle or the sharp point of a fillet knife, focusing on the skin covering the fat and pricking at an angle to avoid piercing the meat on the drumstick and center of the thigh. Sprinkle evenly with the salt. Let stand at room temperature for 50 to 60 minutes.

Pour the oil over the bottom of a small baking dish. Place the duck legs in the oil, arranging them close together but not overlapping. Place in a cold oven. Set the oven to 275 degrees. Bake for 2½ hours or until the duck is cooked through. Let stand to cool for 30 minutes.

Arrange the duck legs on a baking sheet or wire rack of an air fryer. Set the oven or air fryer to 375 degrees; do not preheat. Bake or air fry the duck legs for 15 minutes or until the skin is crisp. Let stand to rest for 5 to 6 minutes before serving.

May reserve the pan drippings in the refrigerator for cooking vegetables or other meats; strain if storing for several weeks or months. May store, tightly covered, for up to 6 months. May store well-wrapped duck meat in the refrigerator for up to 2 weeks.

66 *This is the ultimate low-maintenance luxury dish that results in meltingly tender and flavorful meat.*"

GREEN GODDESS
GRILLED LOBSTER ROLLS

Prep Time: 1¼ to 2¼ hours   **Difficulty:** Medium   **Serves:** 6

INGREDIENTS

2 lobsters

1 tablespoon olive oil

1 teaspoon kosher salt

½ teaspoon freshly ground black pepper

1 cup Green Goddess Dressing (recipe, page 98)

6 slices Texas toast or hot dog buns

Unsalted butter, softened

DIRECTIONS

Bring a large stockpot of water to a boil. Place the lobsters in the water. Boil for 5 minutes. Remove to an ice-water bath to stop the cooking process; drain. Cut the lobsters into halves and remove the green tomalley from the head and tail sections. Crack small sections of the claws and knuckles using a knife to create vents. Brush the lobsters with the olive oil. Season evenly with the salt and pepper.

Preheat the grill to 350 degrees. Place the lobsters on the grill and close the lid. Grill for 2 minutes. Turn the lobsters over. Grill for 2 minutes. Continue this process for 8 to 10 minutes or until the meat is firm and cooked. Remove to a baking sheet. Let stand to rest for 4 to 5 minutes. Chill for 1 to 2 hours.

Remove all of the meat from the lobster tail. Crack the claws and knuckles and remove the meat. Cut the lobster meat into 1-inch pieces and place in a bowl. Add the Green Goddess Dressing and toss to coat.

Toast one side of each slice of the bread with butter on a griddle. Spoon equal portions of the lobster mixture lengthwise down the center of the slices. Fold the slices to make boats and place in small trays to serve.

Laura Rea Dickey's
GRILLED
MUSSELS

FAMILY FAVORITE

Prep Time: 10 minutes   **Difficulty:** Easy   **Serves:** 4

INGREDIENTS

2 pounds mussels

¼ cup olive oil

2 tablespoons minced shallot

1 tablespoon minced garlic

1 teaspoon red pepper flakes

2 tablespoons chopped Italian parsley

1 teaspoon kosher salt

½ teaspoon freshly ground black pepper

½ teaspoon ground coriander

2 lemons

Garlic butter

1 baguette, cut into diagonal slices

DIRECTIONS

Preheat a grill to high using lump charcoal. Place the mussels in a colander and rinse under running water; drain. Remove the beards.

Combine the olive oil, shallot, garlic, red pepper flakes, parsley, salt, pepper, and coriander in a large bowl and whisk to mix well. Cut the lemons crosswise into halves and add to the olive oil mixture. Add the mussels and toss to coat evenly.

Spread garlic butter over each slice of bread. Arrange the mussels in a single layer on the grill. Place the lemons cut sides down on the grill. Place the bread around the perimeter of the mussels. Grill for 2 to 5 minutes or until the mussels open, discarding any unopened mussels. Remove the mussels and lemon halves to a bowl. Remove the garlic bread to a plate.

Tossing the mussels in the shells may seem odd, but as the smoke and heat cook the mussels, it roasts the garlic and onion to enhance the overall flavor. Place the mussels in a bowl and then squeeze the grilled lemon juice over them. All of that flavor dresses the steaming mussels in the shell."

Maja Perušić's
SKAMPI
NA BUZARU

Prep Time: 20 to 25 minutes   **Difficulty:** Easy   **Serves:** 4 to 6

INGREDIENTS

2 tablespoons olive oil

1 small onion, finely chopped

6 garlic cloves, minced

¾ cup dry white wine

½ cup tomato purée, or 2 tablespoons tomato paste plus water

½ teaspoon sea salt

¼ teaspoon freshly ground black pepper

2 pounds 16/20 shrimp, unpeeled or peeled and deveined

⅓ cup chopped fresh parsley

1 tablespoon bread crumbs

DIRECTIONS

Heat the olive oil in a sauté pan over medium-high heat. Add the onion. Cook until tender; do not brown. Add the garlic. Cook for 5 minutes, stirring frequently. Add the wine, tomato purée, salt, and pepper. Bring to a simmer. Add the shrimp. Cook over medium-low heat for 15 to 20 minutes or until the shrimp turn pink; do not overcook. Add the parsley and bread crumbs and toss gently.

❝ *I typically serve this dish with crusty bread, polenta, or rice.*❞

BIG DATA AND BBQ

After Roland, Jr., and Laura Rea were married, Laura was drafted into service in the family business. "As my father-in-law says, 'we really needed someone to deal with the dang computers.'" Laura Rea explains, "I was that someone. A task became a strategy and then a new layer to the barbecue business."

Roland Dickey, Sr., says, "I tell franchisees in Barbecue University that to succeed in business, you have to realize and accept that things change. I speak to every class and explain how I started the company. I really focused on catering and sales and personally opened our original fifteen stores, and if I hadn't realized business was changing and we needed to change, that's where the story would end. I explain it by talking about coffee.

Croatia Development Team

I hated instant coffee. The last time I had instant coffee was in 1969, and it was terrible. I used a percolator to make my coffee. Then in 2011, my son Roland buys me an alien pod thing called a Keurig and tells me I need to drink instant coffee again. I think, 'No way, man. You're nuts.' 'Just try it,' he tells me. 'They've done a lot with coffee since the 60s. It's gourmet, lots of flavors; try it.' I now use the alien pod thing for coffee. Still have the percolator, but I use the pods. If my brother and I hadn't brought my son Roland, Jr., into the company, we wouldn't have grown much beyond the ninety stores we had in 1999, and that's where the story would end again. Roland, Jr., really understood business and how to scale. He knew how to take what I had done and evolve it. Same thing with bringing Laura into the business in 2009. We opened Central with a manual cash register. I carried a flip phone until they wouldn't repair it anymore. Without the technology stuff, that's where the story would have ended again. So, be open to change."

Laura first worked with a data partner to develop what is called Smoke Stack for Dickey's. It's an amalgamation of Cloud and Big Data tools that now serves as the nerve center for the business by pulling all data into one place and making it user-friendly. Smoke Stack is the engine that informs the company on all numbers, metrics, and measures—numbers that used to take a week or even a month to deliver but now reports every fifteen minutes. The system pulls information from all Dickey's restaurants, combines it with information from promotions, food-purchasing patterns, and inventory data, among other things. Did our restaurant in Henderson, Nevada, sell out of ribs at lunch? We can see that now and change the digital advertising for dinner away from ribs. After Smoke Stack, Dickey's went on to create a proprietary POS system named SPARK, custom online ordering systems, an app, and a loyalty program. With the uptick in programming, Laura built a team of developers in the US and Croatia that now builds and manages all of Dickey's technology needs. "When I was demoted to CEO, I needed to find someone much smarter than myself to take the tech reins," Laura Rea says. "Carissa De Santis is a better CIO than I was. That's the right kind of change."

Laura and Carissa work from Croatia for at least a month each year, as Laura has since 2011. You will notice that two family recipes from our Croatian team member Maja Perušić are included in the cookbook.

PINEAPPLE BARBECUE
WHOLE RED SNAPPER

Prep Time: 1 hour   **Difficulty:** Medium   **Serves:** 2 to 4

INGREDIENTS

1 stalk lemon grass

½ cup apple cider vinegar

¼ cup packed brown sugar

1 cup pineapple juice

1 tablespoon sea salt

1 tablespoon red pepper flakes

1 tablespoon minced garlic

1 tablespoon ketchup

2 teaspoons cornstarch

2 tablespoons cold water

Zest and juice of 1 lime

2 (1½-pound) whole red snappers, gills and scales removed

1 teaspoon kosher salt

DIRECTIONS

Mince the lemon grass finely, using only the white part. Combine the vinegar, lemon grass, brown sugar, pineapple juice, and sea salt in a large heavy-bottom saucepan over medium-high heat. Bring to a boil. Add the red pepper flakes, garlic, and ketchup. Boil over medium heat for 5 minutes. Reduce the heat to medium-low. Mix the cornstarch and water in a small bowl. Stir into the lemon grass mixture. Cook over low heat until thickened. Pour into a bowl. Let stand to cool. Stir in the lime zest and juice. Reserve half of the sauce to serve with the fish.

Make 4 or 5 diagonal cuts just to the bone in a crisscross pattern on both sides of the fish. Season with the kosher salt, bending the fish in each direction. Let stand to marinate for 30 minutes.

Preheat the grill to 350 to 400 degrees using mesquite or oak charcoal or pellets. Brush the sauce over both sides of the fish, bending the fish in each direction. Grill, uncovered, for 3 to 4 minutes. Turn the fish over. Brush with the sauce. Grill for 3 to 4 minutes. Brush and grill the fish until caramelized and the juices run clear when the fish is pierced with a knife, turning two additional times. Remove to a plate and serve with the reserved sauce. May prepare the sauce up to 2 days in advance.

Chef Phil Butler's
SALMON
ON A CEDAR PLANK

Prep Time: 20 minutes   **Difficulty:** Easy   **Serves:** 1

INGREDIENTS

1 cedar plank

1 (8-ounce) salmon steak (not the tail section)

1 tablespoon mayonnaise

½ teaspoon finely chopped rosemary

3 or 4 grinds freshly ground black pepper

3 tablespoons Parmesan bread crumbs

1 lemon, cut into halves

DIRECTIONS

Soak the cedar plank in water for 10 minutes or longer. Preheat the grill to 400 to 450 degrees. Place the salmon rounded side up on the cedar plank. Spread the mayonnaise over the top. Sprinkle evenly with the rosemary and pepper. Top with the Parmesan bread crumbs. Place the plank on the grill over direct heat. Place the lemon halves cut sides down over indirect heat. Grill, covered, for 6 to 7 minutes or until the fish is cooked medium and the coating is light brown. Serve the fish with the grilled lemon.

> 66 *Talking to Mr. Dickey, we both discussed unique uses for mayonnaise—his on grilled cheese sandwiches and mine to help crust fish and steak roasts with bread crumbs. Here is a simple but flavorful cedar-plank salmon for the grill.*"

CHIPOTLE-GRILLED REDFISH
WITH CRAB ARUGULA SALAD

Prep Time: 10 minutes   **Difficulty:** Medium   **Serves:** 4

INGREDIENTS

1 teaspoon paprika

1 teaspoon kosher salt

½ teaspoon ground chipotle

½ teaspoon granulated garlic

¼ teaspoon ground coriander

⅛ teaspoon black pepper

4 ounces lump crab meat

2 mini sweet peppers, seeded and cut into thin rings

¼ cup Simple Citrus Vinaigrette (recipe, page 99)

1 lemon, cut into halves

4 (6-ounce) scaled skin-on redfish fillets

1 tablespoon olive oil

3 cups torn arugula

DIRECTIONS

Preheat the grill to medium-high. Combine the paprika, salt, chipotle, granulated garlic, coriander, and black pepper in a small cup and crush using the back of a spoon; mix well.

Combine the crab meat and sweet peppers in a bowl. Add the Simple Citrus Vinaigrette and toss lightly. Let stand to marinate.

Place the lemon halves cut sides down on the grill. Grill for 4 to 5 minutes. Remove to a plate. Season the flesh side of the redfish fillets with the paprika mixture, rubbing in slightly. Brush evenly with the olive oil. Place the fillets flesh sides down on the grill. Grill for 2 minutes or until slightly smoky and darkened. Turn the fillets over carefully with a spatula. Grill with the lid closed for 3 to 4 minutes. Remove to a plate. Remove the skin if desired.

Toss the arugula with the marinated crab and peppers. Divide evenly among 4 salad plates. Top each with a redfish fillet. Cut the lemons into halves and serve with the redfish and salad.

Allison Dickey's
SPAGHETTI
WITH OLIVE OIL & GARLIC

Prep Time: 15 minutes   **Difficulty:** Easy   **Serves:** 4 or 5

INGREDIENTS

1 gallon water

2 tablespoons kosher salt

1 pound spaghetti

7 cloves garlic, minced

½ cup extra-virgin olive oil

2 tablespoons heavy cream

1 teaspoon red pepper flakes

Kosher salt to taste

2 tablespoons chopped Italian flat-leaf parsley

1 cup grated Parmigiano-Reggiano cheese

Extra-virgin olive oil, for serving

DIRECTIONS

Combine the water and 2 tablespoons kosher salt in a large stockpot. Add the spaghetti. Cook according to package directions but for 1½ minutes less. Drain the pasta, reserving 1¼ cups of the pasta water.

Sauté the garlic in ½ cup olive oil in a skillet over medium heat just until the garlic changes color. Add 1 cup of the reserved hot pasta water to the garlic mixture. Whisk in the cream and season with the red pepper flakes and salt to taste. Increase the heat to high. Add the pasta. Cook for 30 seconds, tossing constantly with tongs and adding a few tablespoons more of the reserved hot pasta water to keep the sauce thin. Spoon into a large bowl. Sprinkle with the parsley and Parmigiano-Reggiano cheese. Drizzle with a generous amount of olive oil before serving.

> 66 *This dish defines weeknight cooking, when time is of the essence. It's super tasty (Warren and Cullen give it a thumbs-up), and we can pull it together mostly from pantry ingredients. Spend the extra money for a premium dried spaghetti, and be careful to serve it al dente; don't overcook it!"*

Mr. Dickey's
FETTUCCINE
ALFREDO

FAMILY FAVORITE

Prep Time: 15 minutes   **Difficulty:** Easy   **Serves:** 1

INGREDIENTS

6 ounces fettuccine

4 tablespoons unsalted butter

½ cup freshly grated Parmesan cheese

Salt and freshly ground pepper to taste

DIRECTIONS

Cook the fettuccine in a large pot of salted water according to the package directions. Drain the fettuccine, reserving ¼ cup of the pasta water.

Melt the butter in a saucepan over medium heat. Add the fettuccine and reserved pasta water. Add the Parmesan cheese, stirring constantly with a spoon. Cook until the cheese coats the fettuccine. Remove from the heat. Season with salt and pepper.

" Fettuccine Alfredo—I'm talking about the real Fettuccine Alfredo recipe—has no cream in it. Unbeknownst to Americans, Fettuccine Alfredo is essentially fettuccine pasta with Parmesan, butter, salt, and pepper, preferably a freshly mulled pepper. When I do it, I quite often add olive oil to it as well. That's in addition to, or even instead of, the butter, but that's all it is. I make this constantly for myself. Sometimes I add a few tablespoons of raw frozen peas that I heat up with it. I do not add meat to this recipe nor do I add cream. I've been to Italy twelve times, and I've been to every restaurant in Milan, Rome, Capri, you name it. If you go there and you want Alfredo, they will know you're an American. Also, if you want to use cream, they really know you're an American."

LOW COUNTRY
FOIL

Prep Time: 40 minutes   **Difficulty:** Easy   **Serves:** 2

INGREDIENTS

4 red potatoes

8 ounces shell-on 16/20 shrimp, deveined

8 ounces kielbasa, cut into ¼-inch slices

½ small sweet onion, cut into quarters

2 ears of corn, shucked and broken into halves

2 teaspoons Old Bay Seasoning

½ lemon, cut into ⅛-inch slices

Lager beer

DIRECTIONS

Combine the potatoes and enough cold water to cover in a medium saucepan. Simmer over medium heat for 20 to 25 minutes or until fork tender; drain. Let stand to cool.

Cut two 8x16-inch pieces of heavy-duty foil. Place 2 potatoes, 4 ounces shrimp, 4 ounces kielbasa, and 2 pieces of corn in the center of each piece of foil. Season each grouping with 1 teaspoon Old Bay Seasoning. Add 2 slices of the lemon and a splash of beer over each grouping. Fold the foil to enclose and secure the edges, forming a packet. Place the packets on a baking sheet.

Preheat the oven or grill to 450 degrees. Bake the packets for 12 to 15 minutes or until the shrimp are pink. Serve in the foil packets.

DESSERTS
& CLOSERS

Pit Master Robert Dunning's
VANILLA
CAKE

Prep Time: 40 minutes   **Difficulty:** Medium   **Serves:** 6

INGREDIENTS

1 cup (2 sticks) butter, softened

½ cup vegetable shortening

3 cups sugar

5 large eggs, at room temperature

3 cups all-purpose flour

2 teaspoons baking powder

¼ teaspoon salt

½ cup whole milk, at room temperature

½ cup buttermilk, at room temperature

2 teaspoons vanilla extract

After years of cake successes and flops, I'm confident in this homemade vanilla cake. With its outstanding vanilla flavor, pillowy soft crumb, and creamy vanilla buttercream, this is truly the best vanilla cake I've ever had. And after one bite, I guarantee you'll agree."

DIRECTIONS   Preheat the oven to 350 degrees. Spray three 9-inch cake pans with nonstick baking spray or coat well with shortening or butter and flour. Tap over the sink to remove all excess flour.

Cream the 1 cup butter and ½ cup shortening in a large mixing bowl until light and fluffy. Add the sugar 1 cup at a time, beating until well mixed after each addition. Add the eggs one at a time, beating until well mixed after each addition.

Sift the 3 cups flour, baking powder, and salt into a bowl. Whisk the whole milk, buttermilk, and vanilla extract in a small bowl until blended. Add the flour mixture and milk mixture to the butter mixture and stir gently to mix well. Divide the batter evenly among the prepared cake pans. Bake for 25 to 30 minutes or until a wooden pick inserted near the center of the layers comes out clean. Let stand to cool in the pans for 5 minutes before removing from the pans to a wire rack. Spread with preferred frosting.

TWO TEACHERS

As a young student, Roland Dickey, Jr., struggled with dyslexia. He was smart, but reading and spelling were torturous subjects for him. His folks decided he needed a tutor. In third grade, his first tutor was amazingly supportive and interactive. She took young Roland on errands with her, stopped off for ice cream from time to time, and for all intents and purposes, put Roland's lessons second to his happiness. Roland soaked up the one-on-one attention and loved his time with his reading tutor. His reading, however, didn't improve, so his parents hired another tutor the following year. After just one day's lesson, Roland hated his second tutor. All she ever had him do was work, work, and more work. There were no errands, no ice cream, no television time. He nicknamed her "the mean one," but at the end of the year, he was reading at grade level. Later in life, he realized that he learned very little from his first tutor, and it was the second tutor, "the mean one," who actually taught him to read. By Roland's fifth grade year, he was on level with his peers. Because of his second tutor and the hard work she demanded, his disdain for reading was replaced with a voracious appetite that continues to this day. "I really appreciate my tutor. I give her credit for getting me through school, and I talk to our Barbecue University students about the experience. I always share that in hindsight, there is no shortcut for putting in the work—a lesson that has stayed with me for life. Being respected, effective, and fair is better and more honorable than being liked. Choose your partners, business associates, team members, and employees because they share your long-term goals and your work ethic, never because they make you feel good in the short term."

Roland, Jr., speaking at Battle of the Pitmasters

Roland, Jr., speaking at the 75th Anniversary celebration

Pit Master Joan Dahl's
BANANA
BREAD

Prep Time: 35 minutes   **Difficulty:** Easy   **Serves:** 6 to 8

INGREDIENTS

2¼ cups all-purpose flour

1¼ teaspoons baking powder

1¼ teaspoons baking soda

1 teaspoon kosher salt

⅔ cup unsalted butter, softened

4 overripe bananas, mashed

1⅔ cups sugar

½ cup whole milk

2 eggs

1 teaspoon pure vanilla extract

DIRECTIONS

Preheat the oven to 350 degrees. Spray a 9x13-inch baking pan with nonstick baking spray. Combine the flour, baking powder, baking soda, and salt in a bowl and mix well. Beat the butter and bananas in a mixing bowl until blended. Add the sugar, milk, eggs, and vanilla extract and mix well. Mix in the flour mixture. Spoon into the prepared pan. Bake for 30 minutes or until a wooden pick inserted near the center comes out clean.

> " *You can use a 9×13-inch baking pan or a bundt pan. I think the bundt pan makes the best presentation. Increase cook time to 40 to 45 minutes if using a bundt pan.*"

CARAMEL CRUNCH BROWNIE
WITH SNICKERS

Prep Time: 50 to 60 minutes   **Difficulty:** Medium   **Serves:** 6 to 10

INGREDIENTS

Cold butter, for skillet

½ cup salted butter

2 tablespoons vegetable oil

8 ounces unsweetened chocolate, chopped, or chocolate chips

¾ cup all-purpose flour

¼ teaspoon baking soda

3 large eggs

1 cup packed dark brown sugar

1 teaspoon vanilla extract

1 teaspoon whiskey

1 Snickers® bar, slightly frozen

DIRECTIONS

Preheat a grill or smoker to 250 degrees. Grease a 10-inch cast-iron skillet with cold butter.

Combine the ½ cup butter, vegetable oil, and chocolate in a medium saucepan and place the saucepan on the grill. Grill just until the chocolate is melted, stirring occasionally. Let stand to cool for 5 to 10 minutes. Increase the grill temperature to 375 degrees.

Mix the flour and baking soda in a small bowl. Add the eggs, brown sugar, vanilla extract, and whiskey to the chocolate mixture and whisk until smooth. Add the flour mixture and stir to mix; do not overmix. Pour the mixture into the prepared skillet. Place the skillet on the grill over indirect heat. Grill, covered, for 20 minutes. Chop the Snickers into ¼- to ⅓-inch pieces. Sprinkle evenly over the brownie. Grill for 20 to 25 minutes or until a wooden pick inserted near the center comes out clean. Let stand to cool slightly. Cut into wedges and serve with ice cream.

Sandy Rea's
CHOCOLATE
LAYERED DESSERT

Prep Time: 30 minutes (plus 2 to 3 hours)   **Difficulty:** Easy   **Serves:** 8 to 9

INGREDIENTS

1 cup all-purpose flour

1 cup chopped pecans or other nuts, divided

½ cup unsalted butter, melted

8 ounces cream cheese, softened

1 cup powdered sugar

16 ounces frozen whipped topping, thawed, divided

2 (3-ounce) packages chocolate or chocolate fudge instant pudding mix

4 cups whole milk

DIRECTIONS

Preheat the oven to 350 degrees. Combine the flour, ½ cup of the pecans, and butter in a bowl and mix well. Press over the bottom of a 9x13-inch baking dish. Bake for 15 minutes. Let stand to cool completely.

Beat the cream cheese and powdered sugar in a mixing bowl until blended. Fold in 1 cup of the whipped topping. Spread over the cooled crust.

Combine the pudding mix and milk in a large bowl. Whisk for 2 to 3 minutes or until well mixed. Spread over the cream cheese mixture. Spread the remaining whipped topping over the pudding and sprinkle with the remaining ½ cup pecans. Chill for 2 to 3 hours before serving.

66 *This Chocolate Layered Dessert is perfect for all of the chocolate lovers in your life. It's a fabulous treat to bring to parties and holiday gatherings, and people always ask me for the recipe."*

KEY LIME
ICEBOX PIE

Prep Time: 20 minutes (plus 6 hours)   **Difficulty:** Easy   **Serves:** 6 to 8

INGREDIENTS

1 (3-ounce) package vanilla instant pudding mix

1 cup whole milk

¼ cup plus 2 teaspoons key lime juice, divided

1½ tablespoons (or more) grated lime zest, divided

16 ounces frozen whipped topping, thawed, divided

1½ sleeves graham crackers

DIRECTIONS

Whisk the pudding mix, milk, ¼ cup of the lime juice, and 1 tablespoon of the lime zest in a bowl until smooth. Let stand for 5 to 6 minutes or until slightly set. Fold in 8 ounces of the whipped topping.

Line the bottom of an 8x8-inch dish with graham crackers, breaking to fit if needed. Sprinkle evenly with ½ teaspoon of the lime juice. Spread a third of the pudding evenly over the graham crackers. Add a layer of graham crackers and sprinkle with ½ teaspoon of the lime juice. Spread half of the remaining pudding evenly over the graham crackers. Repeat the layers, ending with graham crackers and lime juice. Spread the remaining 8 ounces whipped topping over the top and sprinkle with remaining ½ tablespoon lime zest. Chill, covered, for 6 hours or overnight. Store any leftovers, loosely covered, in the refrigerator.

BLACKBERRY
SMASH

Prep Time: 3 minutes   **Difficulty:** Easy   **Serves:** 2

INGREDIENTS

15 blackberries

10 large mint leaves

1½ ounces simple syrup

2 ounces fresh orange juice

4 ounces bourbon

Ice

4 ounces club soda (optional)

2 blackberries, for garnish

DIRECTIONS

Muddle 15 blackberries, mint, and simple syrup in a large cocktail shaker. Add the orange juice and bourbon. Fill the shaker with ice and seal tightly. Shake for 30 seconds.

Fill 2 cocktail glasses with crushed ice. Strain the drink into the glasses, dividing evenly. Add 2 ounces club soda to each drink. Garnish each glass with a blackberry.

Lauren Lumbley's
GRAPEFRUIT
PISCO

Prep Time: 5 minutes　　　**Difficulty:** Easy　　　**Serves:** 12

INGREDIENTS

1 cup honey

½ cup water

1 (750-ml) bottle pisco

22 ounces (660 ml) fresh grapefruit juice

11 ounces (330 ml) fresh lime juice

½ teaspoon Cholula or other hot sauce

Ice

6 grapefruit slices, cut into halves, for garnish

Flaky salt, such as Maldon

DIRECTIONS

Combine the honey and water and mix well to make honey syrup. Combine the honey syrup, pisco, grapefruit juice, lime juice, and Cholula in a 2½- to 3-quart pitcher and stir to mix well. Chill, covered, for up to 2 hours. Stir and pour into ice-filled rocks glasses. Garnish each glass with a piece of grapefruit and sprinkle with a pinch of flaky salt.

66 *You can serve this easy-drinking grapefruit cocktail in a punch bowl for the perfect backyard barbecue gathering."*

GRILLED GRAPEFRUIT
PALOMA

Prep Time: 30 minutes   **Difficulty:** Easy   **Serves:** 4

INGREDIENTS

1 pink grapefruit

1 teaspoon kosher salt

1 teaspoon sugar

12 lime wedges, divided

4 tablespoons simple syrup

½ cup blanco tequila

Ice

1½ cups soda water

DIRECTIONS

Preheat the grill to 350 degrees. Cut the grapefruit into ¼-inch half-moons. Grill the grapefruit for 2 minutes per side. Let stand to cool. Combine the salt and sugar on a small plate. Run 1 of the lime wedges around the rim of each glass, reserving each lime wedge to garnish the glass. Press the rim into the salt mixture to coat. To make each drink, muddle 3 slices of the grapefruit and 2 of the lime wedges in a prepared glass. Add 1 tablespoon simple syrup and 2 tablespoons of the tequila. Add ice and a fourth of the soda water and stir. Garnish each glass with a reserved lime wedge. Serve immediately.

CENTRAL BAR, WHERE EVERYBODY— ESPECIALLY GARY—KNOWS YOUR NAME

The Dickey family converted a small house into the first Dickey's Barbecue Pit in 1941. Still serving folks there today, guests can see the original fireplace in the dining room and the original pit in the kitchen. The first Dickey's is the oldest continuously operating restaurant in Dallas, Texas, that has never closed, changed locations, or changed ownership. Short on funds, the Dickey family rented space to Dr Pepper® to pay for the original sign, and the sign has remained on the building ever since. Beer was also on the original menu and has always paired well with barbecue.

Over time, a small side room was used as a to-go counter, but as folks' preferences changed to favor delivery, the space needed to be put to better use, thus Central Bar was born. In 2019, the space was remodeled as a bar. The original restaurant remained, but Central Bar has become a hub of the neighborhood. Laura Rea, along with Aaron Brewer, a key Dickey's team member of twelve years, spent many hours hanging old photos and décor to ensure Central Bar returned to its authentic roots. "I wanted to make sure the bar honored our roots and to create a welcoming little dive bar that went great with barbecue," says Laura Rea. "I also owe a huge thank you to Aaron Brewer, Julie Moore, and Chris Kelley, who saw the vision and helped pull everything together, including the mural outside the bar. Now Chef Phil and Beverage Director Dan Timm keep our regulars happy with rotating craft cocktails. I love this little bar and team."

Gary Stapleton outside original Dickey's location

The result is a local bar that feels as though it has always been there. Gary Stapleton, the Honorary Mayor of Central Bar, is a neighbor and friend, who has taken up frequent residence in the establishment. As a successful business owner, as well as a member of a competition barbecue team, Gary has not only come to love the bar, but the restaurant as well. You'll often find him prepping the line and other chores in the back of house, right alongside employees. His devotion to the brand also has earned him a position on the board of The Dickey Foundation. When you're in town, drop on in and see us. Gary will be there to greet you.

Laura Rea Dickey's
PINK VODKA
LEMONADE PITCHER

Prep Time: 10 minutes (plus 1 hour) **Difficulty:** Easy **Serves:** 8 to 10

INGREDIENTS

2 cups ice

¾ cup vodka, preferably Tito's®

⅓ cup fresh lime juice

¼ cup rum, preferably Malibu®

1¼ quarts good-quality lemonade

1 (12-ounce) can Sprite®

DIRECTIONS

Combine the ice, vodka, lime juice, rum, and lemonade in a large pitcher and mix well. Stir in the Sprite. Serve immediately.

> 66 *This drink is so delightful to enjoy on the beach.*"

VODKA GRAPE
SPARKLER

Prep Time: 10 minutes (plus 1 hour)   **Difficulty:** Easy   **Serves:** 8 to 10

INGREDIENTS

2 pounds fresh red seedless grapes

½ cup clover honey

½ cup fresh lemon juice

¾ cup very cold vodka

1 bottle very cold rosé sparkling wine

DIRECTIONS

Slice enough of the grapes to fill 1 cup. Combine the remaining grapes, honey, and lemon juice in a blender and process until smooth. Pour into a pitcher.

Stir in the vodka and sliced grapes. Chill, covered, for 1 hour or until cold. Add the rosé and stir gently. Serve in thin-walled flutes. May serve over crushed ice.

Aaron Brewer's
RATTLESNAKE MARGARITA

Prep Time: 2 minutes   **Difficulty:** Easy   **Serves:** 1

INGREDIENTS

Lime wedge

Tajín to taste

1 ounce cranberry juice

2½ ounces margarita mix

2 ounces tequila, preferably Casamigos Blanco®

Juice of ¼ lime

Sliced jalapeño pepper to taste

Ice

½ ounce raspberry liqueur

DIRECTIONS

Run the lime wedge around the rim of a glass and dip the rim in Tajín. Shake the cranberry juice, margarita mix, tequila, lime juice, and jalapeño in a cocktail shaker. Pour into an ice-filled glass. Add the liqueur.

> 66 *The Tajín is what makes this drink for me. Grab yourself a nice umbrella and sit by the pool to enjoy this drink."*

66 *It's a holiday anytime this whiskey is served! A month in the making, this cocktail is worth the wait. Whiskey is infused with the flavors of apples, cinnamon, and cloves, all of which are given a smoky oak flavor. A spectacular holiday drink anytime of year."*

Chef Phil Butler's
SMOKED
HOLIDAY WHISKEY

Prep Time: 1 hour (plus 1 month)   **Difficulty:** Easy   **Serves:** 4

INGREDIENTS

8 dried apple rings

2 cinnamon sticks

5 whole cloves

1 teaspoon black pepper

3 tablespoons brown sugar

8 allspice berries

3 tablespoons medium-toasted American oak chips

1 tablespoon dark-toasted American oak chips

1 bottle white corn whiskey

DIRECTIONS

Combine the dried apple rings, cinnamon sticks, cloves, pepper, brown sugar, allspice berries, medium-toasted oak chips, and dark-toasted oak chips in a mixing bowl and mix well.

Preheat a smoker to 180 degrees. Line a baking sheet with foil. Spread the apple ring mixture on the prepared baking sheet. Smoke for 45 minutes. Let stand to cool to room temperature. Pour into a 32-ounce canning jar. Add the whiskey and cover. Shake the jar until the brown sugar is dissolved. Let stand at room temperature for 25 days. Chill for 5 days. Strain into 4 glasses and serve.

MURDER
HORNET

Prep Time: 5 to 6 minutes   **Difficulty:** Easy   **Serves:** 6

INGREDIENTS   3 ounces honey whiskey   3 ounces frozen Fireball Cinnamon Whisky®

DIRECTIONS   Stack 10 to 15 hickory wood chips on the back side of a large sauté pan or a piece of steel. Place a handful of large ice cubes in a 16- to 20-ounce glass. Pour the honey whiskey and Fireball Cinnamon Whiskey® over the ice. Stir with a long spoon to chill the beverage and melt some of the ice. Strain into 6 shot glasses.

Arrange the glasses in a honeycomb pattern next to the chips on the back of the sauté pan. Light the wood chips using a blow torch; do not light the beverages. Place a cake dome over the glasses and fire. Let stand to smoke for 1 minute. Remove the cake dome and serve the shots immediately.

NOTE   *Full disclosure: Your cakes might start to smell a little smoky after making this drink. Once you taste it, however, you may agree that your cake dome has found a new purpose in life. The name is based on the ingredients and how the six shots—all lined up—look like a honeycomb. Beware, they do bite after a few.*

SMOKY
OG

Prep Time: 5 to 6 minutes   **Difficulty:** Easy   **Serves:** 1

INGREDIENTS

1 Luxardo Cherry®

1 (2-inch) orange peel strip

2 dashes of orange bitters

½ teaspoon Luxardo Cherry® syrup

½ ounce simple syrup

1½ ounces Woodford Reserve Bourbon Whiskey®

Ice

DIRECTIONS

Stack 10 to 15 hickory wood chips on the back side of a large sauté pan or a piece of steel. Muddle the cherry and orange peel 2 or 3 times in the bottom of a rocks or old-fashioned glass. Add the orange bitters, cherry syrup, simple syrup, and whiskey to the cherry mixture. Add ice. Stir with a spoon to chill the beverage. Place the glass next to the wood chips on the back of the sauté pan. Light the wood chips using a blow torch; do not light the beverage. Place a cake dome over the glass and fire. Let stand to smoke for 1 minute. Remove the cake dome and serve the shot immediately.

NOTE

A good-quality bourbon whiskey and a marinated cherry are musts in this drink recipe. The smoke and Luxardo Cherry make this libation one that you will want to sip all night, while cooking that brisket. Use a 2-inch square ice cube to ensure that the bourbon will not get too watered down.

Pit Master Josh Wise's
DICKEY'S SIGNATURE
GREEN TEA

PIT MASTER APPROVED

Prep Time: 1 minute   **Difficulty:** Easy   **Serves:** 1

INGREDIENTS

1 ounce Jameson Irish Whiskey®

¼ ounce peach schnapps

¼ ounce sweet and sour mix

Ice

¼ ounce Sprite®

DIRECTIONS

Combine the Irish whiskey, peach schnapps, and sweet and sour mix in an ice-filled cocktail shaker and shake. Pour into a shooter glass. Top with the Sprite and serve.

66 *The first time I had a green tea shot, it reminded me of a kamikaze because of its yellowish green color and fruity flavor. But while the kamikaze has a strong vodka taste, the green tea shot is much more mellow in the sense that it tastes more like a summer cocktail than a shot."*

TEXAS
TEA

Prep Time: 2 minutes   **Difficulty:** Easy   **Serves:** 1

INGREDIENTS

1½ ounces vodka, preferably Tito's®

¾ ounce orange liqueur, preferably Grand Marnier®

1½ ounces fresh tea

¾ ounce sour mix

1 dash of honey

Ice

1 lemon wedge

DIRECTIONS

Combine the vodka, orange liqueur, tea, sour mix, and honey in an ice-filled cocktail shaker and shake. Strain into a glass of ice. Garnish with the lemon wedge.

Aaron Brewer's
HILL COUNTRY
HIBISCUS TEA

Prep Time: 25 minutes (plus 30 to 60 minutes) **Difficulty:** Easy **Serves:** 4

INGREDIENTS

5 cups water

½ cup loose hibiscus tea leaves

1 cup chopped fresh strawberries

10 mint leaves

2 to 3 tablespoons honey

Ice

Strawberries, lime wedges, and fresh mint, for garnish

DIRECTIONS

Boil the water in a medium pot over high heat. Add the hibiscus leaves. Remove from the heat. Add the 1 cup strawberries, 10 mint leaves, and honey. Mash the strawberries gently. Let the tea steep for 20 minutes.

Pour the tea through a fine-mesh strainer into a glass pitcher; chill.

Fill the pitcher with ice. Fill 4 glasses with ice and garnish with strawberries, lime wedges, and mint. Pour the tea into the glasses. May serve with additional honey if desired.

> 66 *Have yourself a karaoke dance party and enjoy this smooth Hill Country Hibiscus Tea with your best girl gang.*"

THE ICONIC BIG YELLOW CUP WASN'T ALWAYS YELLOW

In the 1980s, the Dickeys had an idea that instead of serving iced teas and soft drinks in glassware, they could offer 32-ounce plastic cups that guests would take home with them and keep in their cupboards. The first cups were white and very well received. Then, in 1988, the manufacturer shipped yellow cups by mistake. At first, this obviously was upsetting; however, rather than waiting on a reprint, they decided the yellow cups fit the brand better than the white ones. It's been the Big Yellow Cup ever since.

For rare special occasions, the color of the Big Yellow Cup will change. The 75th anniversary cup was black and gold. During three summers, specially designed yellow traveling cups invited folks to share photos of their traveling cup while on vacation. In October 2019, Dickey's Barbecue Pit joined the fight against breast cancer with the debut of its first limited-edition Pink Big Yellow Cup. With this cup, in partnership with The Dickey Foundation, the pink cup raised $45,000 in funds, which were used to provide mammograms and other breast-cancer detection, treatments, and

services for local first responders. This idea, like many, came from strong partnership. Joan Dahl, an outstanding Dickey's Owner/Operator and past president of the Pit Owners Association (POA), collaborated with Laura Rea Dickey on the pink cup. It was a literal and symbolic success that is now an annual October tradition.

To commemorate the Dickey's eightieth anniversary, they're producing six collectible Big Yellow Cups. "Someday, they might be in the Smithsonian," Mr. Dickey said. "So you better stop in and complete your collection."

Special Edition Black Big Yellow Cup, #ShowUsYourCup

Sybil Huntington's
SMOKY 'TINI

Prep Time: 2 minutes   **Difficulty:** Easy   **Serves:** 1

INGREDIENTS

Ice

2½ ounces London Dry Gin®

¼ ounce Islay Scotch Whiskey® (preferably Ardbeg or Laphroaig)

1 lemon, for garnish

DIRECTIONS

Fill a martini glass with ice and water to chill the glass. Combine the gin, whiskey, and a large ice cube in a high-sided glass and stir with a spoon until well chilled; do not use small ice cubes or flaked ice. Pour the ice water out of the martini glass, shaking out any excess water. Strain the gin mixture into the glass.

Peel the yellow part of the lemon. Twist the peel over the drink and rub the lemon peel around the edge of the glass before dropping it into the drink. Share with someone you love. Engagement ring optional!

NOTE

Sybil's Smoky 'Tini is a recipe for romance. The classic martini has a long legacy of history and hype. With this personal variation, I'm adding my own true narrative. It is a tale of perfect pairings and passions pursued. Once upon a time, a chill, crisp, floral gin met a smoky, savory, peaty Scotch whiskey, and the magic began. At least it did for me that evening when the man of my dreams proposed marriage over this Smoky 'Tini love potion, garnished with

his grandmother's diamond ring in addition to the classic lemon zest. I guess our own love story (still being written) affirms the adage "Where there is smoke, there is fire." Are you not yet dazzled by the flames of passion? Take comfort—rest assured this potent potable is a perfect partner for Dickey's slow-smoked, spicy ribs or savory, flame-kissed lamb rib chops from your own wood grill or smoker. Stoke those embers and join me in raising a Smoky 'Tini toast to life's most noble pursuits—Peace, Love, and Barbecue.

Jeff Gruber's
BARBECUE
BLOODY MARY

Prep Time: 5 to 6 minutes　　　**Difficulty:** Easy　　　**Serves:** 3

INGREDIENTS

14 ounces V8® spicy vegetable juice

2 ounces Dickey's Original Barbecue Sauce

3 teaspoons horseradish

1½ ounces vodka, preferably Tito's®

½ teaspoon Dickey's Chili Pork Butt Rub

½ teaspoon Worcestershire sauce

Juice of ½ lemon

Ice

½ lemon, cut into halves

Dickey's Chili Pork Butt Rub, for glass

Hot brisket burnt ends, ribs, shrimp, sausage, celery sticks, and pickled jalapeño peppers, for garnish

DIRECTIONS

Combine the vegetable juice, Dickey's Original Barbecue Sauce, horseradish, vodka, Dickey's Chili Pork Butt Rub, Worcestershire sauce, and lemon juice in a pitcher with ice and mix well. Run the lemon around the rim of each of 3 glasses and dip in Dickey's Chili Pork Butt Rub. Fill each glass with the beverage.

Thread brisket burnt ends, ribs, shrimp, and sausage on 3 skewers and place in the beverages. Add celery sticks and pickled jalapeños and serve.

> Here's a time saver: Food and beverage in the same glass! This Bloody Mary contains, among other things, Dickey's Original Barbecue Sauce and Dickey's Chili Pork Butt Rub. The cocktail is garnished with barbecue burnt ends, ribs, shrimp, sausage, and, of course, celery. A great breakfast eye-opener!"

EPILOGUE

"Family," from our perspective, is a really big word. Everyone that has helped make Dickey's "the biggest little barbecue joint" in the world is part of our family. We love barbecue. We love the business of barbecue. And we love folks who share our barbecue passion and profession.

Hopefully, this cookbook expresses our great appreciation for good food and our gratitude toward everyone *Behind the BBQ.* We also hope you found it interesting, insightful, and often humorous to see and hear from the folks that call Dickey's home.

When you've made your career in barbecue, you certainly have more good days than bad. As the third generation leading Dickey's Barbecue, we're proud and humbled that Dickey's has grown from that one little restaurant in Dallas to the largest barbecue restaurant corporation in the world. We also are intimately focused on ensuring that when a guest sits down at any of our restaurants around the world, their entire experience is uniquely Dickey's—authentic Texas barbecue and genuine service that will bring them back time and time again. That's what gets us up in the morning.

That focus on authentic, quality barbecue in our restaurants is what has led us to bring so many parts of the barbecue business "in house"—from sauce and spice production to guest technology to barbecueathome.com to craft sausage making. We see our mission as protecting, preserving, and serving the highest quality Texas barbecue to as many folks as we can every day. We endeavor to honor our legacy while building our future so the Dickey family is still serving Legit Texas Barbecue for another eighty years. We aim to work every day to accomplish this, with good folks and a sense of humor, while doing both well and good in our communities. Our commitment to the great barbecue experience is also why we've written this cookbook to celebrate Dickey's eightieth anniversary.

We are so very pleased to share our last name with this company, which has so many wonderful stories to tell. We hope you've enjoyed reading them intermingled in the pages of our family recipes. Yes, they may be Texas tall tales, but we can assure you that all of them are (mostly, probably) true.

From our family to yours, we thank you for being our guest. Please come back, bring a friend, and dine with us again.

Best Sauce & Good Burnt Ends,
Laura Rea Dickey, CEO of Dickey's Barbecue Restaurants, Inc.
with Roland Dickey, Jr., CEO of Dickey's Capital Group

CONTRIBUTOR BIOS

Mr. Roland Dickey is the son of Travis Dickey, founder of Dickey's Barbecue Pit. Roland was a senior at SMU, planning a career in law, when he stepped in to run the family restaurant upon his father's passing in 1967. He took the single barbecue stand and expanded throughout the Dallas–Fort Worth area with the support of his wife and brother. Roland developed many of Dickey's original recipes, started the legendary catering program, and sold the first franchise in 1994 to the Smiths, who are still franchisees today. He built Dickey's from a single restaurant to twelve family-owned stores and

Greer Martin, Roland, Laura Rea, Roland, Jr., Chef Phil Butler, and Aaron Brewer attending a food demonstration for Fox & Friends at Super Bowl LIV

Roland with Laura Rea

then grew the business to ninety restaurants with franchise partners. In 1999, he and his brother asked his son Roland Dickey, Jr., to leave his restaurant role outside the company and join the family business; he then passed the head Pit Master title to his son in 2006, who took his place as CEO. Roland, Sr., published his cookbook, *Mr. Dickey's Barbecue Cookbook*, in 2012. He is a member of the Board of Directors for Dickey's Capital Group, the board for the family businesses. When he is not enjoying his condo in Florida, Mr. Dickey visits Owner/ Operators, hosts appreciation events, makes special appearances on local radio and television shows, and ensures our guests enjoy their low and slow– smoked Texas-style barbecue over a tall tale.

Maurine Dickey, Dickey family matriarch, has dedicated her life to serving her community, including serving eight years as a Dallas County Commissioner and serving as Chairman of the Parkland Hospital Board. While a Commissioner, Maurine was very involved in regional issues, such as transportation and high-speed rail. She represented Dallas County on the North Central Texas Council of Governments' Regional Transportation Commission, as well as serving on the COG's Board of Directors. She chaired the County's Clean Air Task Force and served as the Vice President of the Texas High-Speed Rail Company.

Cullen, Roland, Sr., Maurine, and Roland, Jr., with Maurine's mother, Ms. Petty

In the aftermath of the deadly downtown Dallas shooting in 2016, Maurine channeled her passion for helping those who protect and serve by creating The Dickey Foundation. Since then, the Foundation has helped countless first responders with protective armor, firefighting equipment, and other essential gear so they can safely do their jobs. She also is passionate about helping children, having chaired the Texas Department of Protective and Regulatory Services, an agency that is devoted to the protection of children, as well as chairing the Dallas County Child Welfare Board and helping found CPS Community Partners. Maurine is a member of the Board of Directors for Dickey's Capital Group, the board for the family businesses.

Married for more than fifty-five years after meeting at Southern Methodist University, Maurine and Roland Dickey have two sons.

Cullen Dickey learned to value hard work while growing up in Dickey's restaurants and kitchens. While his father, Roland Dickey, Sr., instilled a love of barbecue and cooking in Cullen, he also taught Cullen about commercial real estate as they bought properties and grew their restaurants across Dallas. After graduating from SMU, Cullen was bitten by

Maurine Dickey

the real estate bug and has more than two decades of commercial real estate experience, including founding his own firm, Dickey Property Company, in 2013. Even in his commercial real estate business, he embodies the Dickey's value of "Do Both Well and Good" as he provides unmatched local knowledge, a deep network of Dallas business relationships, and a commitment to helping the community. Cullen is a member of the Board of Directors for Dickey's Capital Group, the board for the family businesses. Cullen and his wife, Allison, have a wonderful son, Warren, and can often be found cheering Warren on from the sidelines at his various sporting events or sourcing hard-to-find ingredients to create the perfect family meal at home.

before coming back to Dickey's in 1999. He worked his way up in restaurant operations to serve as CEO of Dickey's Barbecue Restaurants, Inc., until 2017. Seeing the need to better support franchisees and preserve quality, he vertically integrated the company, expanding support specialties into independent companies. He now serves as CEO of Dickey's Capital Group.

Roland Dickey, Sr., as a child

Roland Dickey, Jr., is the Chief Executive Officer of Dickey's Capital Group, the holding company of Dickey's Barbecue Restaurants, Inc. The grandson of the company's founder, Roland, Jr., began working for the family brand early on, learning the craft of the family's smoking process from his dad. He graduated from Southern Methodist University and achieved success working for El Chico Restaurants

Renee Roozen, Aaron Brewer, Carissa De Santis, Jeff Gruber, Laura Rea, and Roland, Jr.

During his time as CEO of the restaurant brand, Roland, Jr., has expanded Dickey's Barbecue from 90 locations to more than 500 locations. Roland, Jr., created Dickey's signature Jalapeño Cheddar Sausage, added macaroni and cheese to the menu, evolved the branded from buffet service to fast causal, streamlined the restaurant size from 5,000 square feet

Roland, Jr., with the ladies of Dickey's

to 2,000 square feet to increase profitability and scalability, opened the first international location in Dubai, and focused on creating an extensive training program to ensure quality barbecue for every guest. Roland, Jr., truly scaled and modernized the barbecue business, while preserving Dickey's authentic quality.

Roland, Jr., saw the opportunity that being the world's largest barbecue brand presented, opting to bring outsourced services in-house for quality and integrity assurance. He opened Wycliff Douglas to make Dickey's sauces and spices and produce products for other restaurant brands. He began Dickey's retail business, placing the brand's products in grocery stores. He opened Stanford Sonoma and restaurantequipmentonline.com to

Roland, Jr., with Kelley Anne

manufacture and sell restaurant equipment and custom furniture and finish-out services. He launched Barbecue at Home by Dickey's, an online barbecue subscription service, which offers guests barbecue, steaks, sides, and meals to heat and serve at home.

He launched Dickey's Craft Sausage Company to make all of Dickey's signature sausages and offer more than twenty varieties of handcrafted, small-batch kielbasa sausages direct to guests online. Roland, Jr., sees his mission as protecting, preserving, and expanding his family's Legit Texas Barbecue legacy and the Dickey brand. In his "spare time," Roland is a major history buff, loves reading business books, adores his three dogs, and is passionate about spending time with his wife and traveling. He also loves fast cars.

Laura Rea Dickey currently serves as Chief Executive Officer of Dickey's Barbecue Restaurants, Inc. She has been serving the brand since 2009 and most recently served as Chief Information Officer before transitioning to CEO in 2017. With over twenty years of experience in marketing, communications, and technology, Laura Rea has helped ensure that the barbecue brand evolves. In her time as CEO, Laura Rea has continued the company's positive trajectory, achieving both record same-stores sales wins and growing the brand to over 600 US locations. She has opened Dickey's kitchens so guests can see the real barbecue pits at work, focused on menu innovations, and temporarily turned the Big Yellow Cup pink in October 2020 to support breast cancer screenings for first responders. As CIO, Laura Rea implemented a new technology infrastructure for the brand, bringing big data to barbecue in 2015 by building Smoke Stack, which was profiled for its technological innovation by *Forbes* and *The Wall Street Journal*. She also has led development of several technology projects, including a proprietary Point-Of-Sale System, Online Ordering System, Loyalty Program, App, and Inventory Management System. The pandemic of 2020 put unique pressure on the restaurant industry, and the brand's technology distinguished itself when Laura Rea launched an upgraded e-commerce site in April 2020, with online traffic growing 122 percent. Laura Rea also has launched new revenue streams for

Laura Rea with Dickey's Owner/Operator Andre Bushell

the company, adding three virtual concepts and an online barbecue subscription service, called Barbecue at Home by Dickey's. Serving as the brand's spokesperson, Laura Rea often appears on national and local television segments, as well as conducting magazine and podcast interviews. As a Wyoming native, raised in Oklahoma, and a TCU graduate, she enjoys being the lone horned frog in a Texas family of SMU mustangs. When she's not talking barbecue, Laura Rea enjoys reading, horseback riding, chasing her twin pugs, traveling, and of course, going to restaurants.

Dickey family Christmas dinner: Roland, Sr., slicing the ham at Elizabeth Mills' home

Laura Rea, Carissa De Santis, and Aaron Brewer

Elizabeth Dickey Mills is the daughter of Dickey's Barbecue founder Travis D. Dickey, Sr., and sister and aunt to the two Roland Dickeys. Very soon after her father's death in 1967, she joined her mother, Ollie Rich Dickey, in the Dickey's

Elizabeth Mills with brother, Roland Dickey, Sr.

Office to help with payroll and general office tasks. She was invaluable to the progress of Dickey's Barbecue Restaurants, Inc. After retiring in the late 1980s, Elizabeth became a community volunteer in numerous pursuits, serving on several hospital boards and at juvenile detention centers, working in literacy in a local men's prison and Hutchins State Jail, and serving on the Texas State Board for Mentally Challenged Offenders. Elizabeth's passion to volunteer has always been extremely important to her, and she served with a high degree of enthusiasm and dedication. When she isn't spending time with her family and five grandchildren, she is leading her local adult Bible study and visiting the gym on a regular basis.

Sandy and Dennis Rea met at the University of Central Oklahoma in Edmond, Oklahoma. After graduation, they married and made

Kelley Anne, Carmen Miranda, and Charro, Roland, Jr., and Laura Rea's dogs

their home in Oklahoma City, where Sandy had a successful career working for Oklahoma Governor David Hall and then running USA Insurance Network with MC and Jo Duncan before retirement. She also ran her own interior design business and decorated Montana Mike's restaurants across the country. Dennis was passionate about his community and served the State of Oklahoma as Director of the Board of Private Vocational Schools for more than thirty years. Together, they have two children, daughter Laura Rea Dickey and son Patrick Rea. They enjoy spending family time with Laura and her husband, Roland Dickey, Jr., as well as Patrick and his wife, Roxie Stiles, and their three grandchildren, James Aidan Rea, Kinzlee Rea, and Kennedy Rea.

Nota McCulley was the culinary heart of the Rea family and a beloved grandmother to Laura Rea Dickey and mother to her only child, Sandy Rea. She spent much of her time working at Tinker Air Force Base in Oklahoma and was one of seven children. Nota and all five of her sisters' names begin with the letter N, and they often were fondly called the great Aunt NuhNuhNuhs to make it easier on everyone. Nota and her husband, Vernon, lived in Choctaw, Oklahoma, where you would occasionally see Nota on her John Deere riding mower well into her late eighties. Before her passing at the age of ninety, Nota shared her southern cooking at weekly family dinners and holidays.

Joanna Windham is a longtime friend of the brand—since the late 1990s. She has an extensive background in restaurants and public relations. Spending much of her time in New York City as a former model for Kim Dawson, she opened Joanna's Restaurant in New York City in the 1980s and was part of the early Southwest Airlines advertising campaigns before opening her own public relations business in Dallas. Joanna consulted for Dickey's when the restaurants started expanding and voiced many of Dickey's early radio commercials. She also appeared with Mr. Dickey in early TV commercials, playing a variety of characters. She's a small-town Texas gal with big-city smarts, who is known to bring laughter, wit, and authenticity to her work.

Aaron Brewer, Spencer Mahoney, Laura Rea, and Greer Martin

Dickey's video and production team with Laura Rea

MJ Breaux started as a loyal Dickey's guest, whose passion for our barbecue led to his purchasing the original franchised location in Mesquite in 2006. Since then, his location is consistently one of the strongest in the country, which he credits to his relationship with local schools, sports teams, churches, and other community organizations. Loyalty is one of the keys to his success, and he never takes for granted his strong relationship with Mesquite ISD, where he serves more than 10,000 meals each year.

Aaron Brewer is the travel-team captain and executive assistant to Dickey's CEO, Laura Rea Dickey. Her organizational skills make her a critical part of the travel team as she often can be found on the road with both Laura Rea and Roland Dickey, Sr., serving as an enthusiastic champion for the brand. When not being a road warrior, Aaron is a fabulous hostess, who can be found entertaining her family and friends around the firepit or hosting an epic dance party.

Carissa, Laura Rea, Aaron, and Gary at Central Bar

Chef Phil Butler, Dickey's Barbecue Pit Research and Development Chef, has over thirty years of experience in the restaurant industry, but he began his culinary journey with Legit Texas Barbecue in August of 2018. His passion for the restaurant industry began in his teens, and he later went on to develop his skills at the Culinary School of America in New York. Chef Phil's work has been featured at many events and in multiple publications, including the James Beard House and *Bon Appétit* magazine. When Chef Phil isn't behind the block, managing the pit, or creating new recipes, he enjoys using his free time to train, race bicycles, and travel the world. He enjoys cooking and spending time with his beautiful wife, Audrey, and two highly active kids, Keira and Damian.

Chef Phil Butler and David Schmidt working the line

Laura Rea standing on her designated pot with Chef Phil for a remote TV segment. Fun fact: Chef Phil is over 6'5" tall!

Dickey's Christmas in July Table Decoration Winners

Remote TV segment crew

Shannon Bullock is the Vice President of Operations for Dickey's Barbecue Pit and supports more than 550 locations by managing the Community Marketing Managers and Regional Business Leaders. She's been with the brand for more than three years and is passionate about driving sales and pushing the team to be results oriented with a sense of urgency. When she's not in the field or on the phone speaking with Owner/Operators, she enjoys her downtime with her husband of twenty-one years and their twelve-year-old daughter at a Fort Worth Brahmas hockey game.

Joan Dahl, a Michigan native, spent nearly two decades as a successful entrepreneur, including two Dickey's Barbecue Pit locations near Grand Rapids. Drawn to Dickey's by our amazing food, Joan's stores embodied the Dickey's vibe and brand. Before her retirement in 2021, Joan was very involved in the Dickey's Pit Owners Association and other Owner/ Operator leadership committees. Proof that you're always part of the Dickey's family is that Joan is still seen visiting her stores to get that Legit Texas Barbecue that drew her to Dickey's in the first place.

Carissa De Santis is the Chief Information Officer for Dickey's Barbecue Restaurants, Inc., and oversees all company technology platforms. Ms. De Santis has over twenty years of experience in the restaurant industry in both operations and technology and previously served in various leadership roles with other industry brands. She has been recognized by multiple high-level, national publications for her many achievements and innovative ideas. Her awards wall is full, as well. When Carissa isn't managing the technological success of the brand, she loves being home on her ranch, riding horses, caring for her animals, and spending time with her husband.

Simone Dominguez is the Director of Construction for Dickey's Barbecue Pit and has built more than 250 Dickey's Barbecue locations. When she's not building the Dickey's Barbecue empire, she enjoys exploring the

Carissa De Santis, Marijan Lovric, Laura Rea, and Jelena Frlan

Shayla Partusch and Aaron Brewer cheering on live remote TV segment

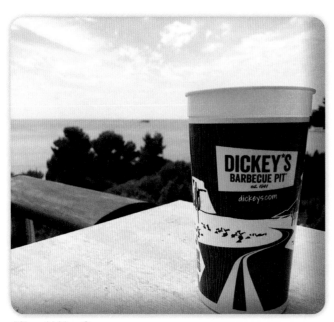

#ShowUsYourCup

Andre Thursby, Dickey's Owner/Operator Krage Fox, and Simone Dominguez

DFW culinary scene, boating, and enjoying live music with her husband, Thomas. Simone embodies the edge, problem solving, and positivity it takes to be a successful woman in construction and barbecue.

Robert Dunning knows about facing challenges from his more than two decades with the United States Marine Corps, so after retiring, he dove headfirst into franchising at Dickey's Barbecue Pit. He has become one of our most successful owners, growing his Louisiana empire from one store to ten Dickey's Family Brand stores in less than ten years. Robert brought Legit Texas Barbecue to New Orleans and credits much of his success to a great Pit Crew and our low-and-slow brisket.

Carissa De Santis and Renee Roozen

Owen Edwards started his journey with Dickey's Barbecue Pit as a teenager back in the summer of 1973 when his mother, who worked in one of our stores, needed his help to fill in as a dishwasher. He came in that day and has never turned back. Diligently working his way from dishwasher to store manager, Owen quickly learned and perfected our brand practices. In 1994, he left the store to serve as Dickey's Director of Operations, helping with new store openings and team training. He now holds a position at Dickey's subsidiary brand Wycliff Douglas. As a lifelong team member and close friend of the Dickey family, not only does he have many stories to tell, but also he's an extremely respected and valued member of the team. In his downtime, Owen enjoys fishing for relaxation and spending time with his three daughters and grandchild.

Remote TV segment crew during COVID-19

Tom Eggerud is a catering guru in Eagan, Minnesota, and has been with the brand since 2010. His passion for Texas-style barbecue is a family affair with his kids working alongside him at the restaurant. He prides himself on growing his business by staying consistent and providing guests high-quality slow-smoked barbecue day in and day out.

Mr. Dickey's TV segment in San Diego

Jeff Gruber serves as Senior Vice President of Dickey's Barbecue Restaurants, Inc., where he handles all of Dickey's franchise relations and focuses on creating positive relationships between the Dickey's Home Office and every Owner/Operator. Although previously working as an attorney, Gruber couldn't resist our hickory-smoked barbecue and began his career with Dickey's in 2008. He has led a large variety of initiatives in multiple departments across the company. His extensive knowledge and commitment to the brand make Jeff a very valuable member of our team. When Gruber isn't charming Owner/Operators, he enjoys playing music, traveling out to West Texas, and spending time with his family.

Laura Rea, Jeff Gruber, and Shayla Partusch filming an infomercial for Dickey's Owner/Operators

Trinity Hall currently serves as President of Stanford Sonoma Corporation, where she leads the charge for the brand's product innovation and oversees the design and construction of all projects internationally. Before taking over at Stanford Sonoma, Trinity spent over ten years in a Senior Vice President role for Dickey's Barbecue Restaurants, Inc., leading franchise sales and managing the opening of more than 550 Dickey's locations across the nation. When Trinity isn't dominating the world of stainless steel fabrication and custom millwork, she loves motorcycles (she is a former dirt bike racer), building and fixing things with her plethora of tools, traveling, spending time with her family, and a cold beer on a warm patio.

Trinity Hall, Aaron Brewer, Shannon Santos, and Laura Rea at the original Dickey's location

Roland, Jr., with Laura Rea at Ernst and Young 2015 Entrepreneur of the Year award

#ShowUsYourCup

Jamie Henretta is the Creative Director for Dickey's Barbecue Restaurants, Inc. She is a creative brand builder and brand historian and applies integrated marketing communication principles to all things within Dickey's Family of Brands. Jamie has a passion for international travel, culture, local cuisine, and the Buffalo Bills, all of which she shares with her husband, travel buddy, personal chef, and treasure man, Brian Henretta, in their Oak Cliff home with two fur children, Amina and Tre'Davious.

Ed Herman currently holds the title of Senior Vice President of Operations at Dickey's Barbecue Restaurants, Inc. He joined the Dickey's family in 2013, serving as a Franchise Director before transitioning into his current senior role. His extensive knowledge

Jamie Henretta

of the restaurant industry, as well as Dickey's brand operations and practices make him vital to the success of our team and also the success of our Owner/Operators. When Ed isn't overseeing our field team and Owner/Operators, he enjoys spending time with his wife of thirty-five years, Teresa, his two amazing daughters, Jennifer and Sandi, and Sandi's husband, Tim, and being a grandad to Brecken and Sutton. Ed is also passionate about traveling, fishing, and discovering hole-in-the-wall restaurants.

Randy Hubbard is one of many long-standing employees at Dickey's, having joined the company as a second-generation team member. Randy's father and Roland Dickey, Sr., worked alongside each other for many years, servicing catering events around Dallas, Texas, in the early years. After his father had a stroke, Randy came on full-time with the company and still works for Dickey's today. When he isn't greeting guests at the chopping block, Randy is passionate about giving back to his community and mentoring others to achieve their dreams. He enjoys spending time with his wife, Bridgett, and daughters, Lakiesha and Jasmine, and taking his grandsons, Darrell and Derek, to the ice cream shop.

Sybil Huntington is an internationally acclaimed writer, restauranteur, and raconteur. Her wise and witty work appears regularly in various print and electronic media, including syndicated radio as "That Wine-ing Woman." When not on the "Eats Beat" or at her Italian farmhouse, she serves as the Honorary Official Greeter at the original Dickey's Barbecue Pit in Dallas, Texas.

Lauren Lumbley is the Senior Director of Franchise Relations and Communications for Dickey's Barbecue Restaurants, Inc., where she works closely with

Dickey's Christmas in July Celebration

internal and external stakeholders to craft brand communications and drive results for Owner/Operators. She is a brand champion, who is often tapped to spearhead critical projects (like this cookbook!), and her determination always results in successful outcomes that are showpieces for the brand. On the off chance she has free time, she is likely to be found on her boat with her husband, JC, and her rescue dogs, Murphy and Pearl. Or she's stealing Betsy's wine at the office.

Jermaine Martin is an IT professional by day, managing teams and getting the job done. At night, his creative side takes over, and he becomes a writer, going by the name J. R. Martin. He loves relaxing with his family and coming up with new stories and recipes for his family to enjoy.

When he's not at his computer solving all the IT problems of the world, you can find him at his computer, creating new problems for his characters to solve.

Lauren Lumbley and Aaron Brewer on the patio at the original Dickey's location

Michelle Matthews is an Executive Sales Leader with a passion to develop and implement strong sales processes to drive significant growth for the business. During her time with the Dickey's brand, she consistently exceeded targets by ensuring best practices across the nation, and international sales goals were met through strategic business development efforts. As an industry leader, she continues to lead through public-speaking engagements to educate, lead, and deliver messaging to lead network growth. She is an

Back row: Roland, Jr., Maurine Dickey, Roland Dickey, Sr., Cullen's wife, Allison, and Cullen Dickey
Front row: Cullen and Allison's son, Warren, and Roland, Jr.'s wife, Laura Rea

avid Louisville fan and is an experienced bourbon connoisseur, who grew up in Kentucky. Michelle and her husband, Ryan, enjoy catching some rays on a beach, wine tasting, and spending time with their two little kids and fur babies.

Julie Moore, better known as "Jules," has worked with Dickey's Barbecue Restaurant, Inc., for the past three years in various roles under the guidance and leadership of the mighty Training Department. She believes that continued education and support is key for owners to maintain a competitive edge in this dynamic environment. In addition to her training roles, she has had the opportunity to work within focused teams on several top-line projects to diligently guide them to completion. Before and after the timeclock starts, her time happily is consumed by cooking, gardening, Pilates, pups, the beach, family, and friends.

Dickey's Owner/Operator Harry Chauhan with Laura Rea, Mr. Dickey, and Carissa De Santis

Filming with Laura Rea, Betsy Orton, and Chef Phil Butler

Ollie Rich, Travis Dickey, Sr.'s wife

Aaron Brewer, Shayla Partusch, and Trinity Hall

Jerry Murray, brand strategist, copywriter, and producer, helps Dickey's Barbecue Restaurants, Inc., set the course for creative marketing initiatives and works closely with the Marketing Department to bring them to life. His friendship with the Dickey family began with Laura Rea Dickey, who worked for him just after she graduated from college. Jerry's mission is to help grow the Dickey's brand through the power and energy of intelligent creative campaigns—and to someday be able to smoke a brisket like Chef Phil.

Betsy Orton is the Executive Director of The Dickey Foundation, where she uses her passion for barbecue and philanthropy to help first responders. Under her guidance, the Foundation has grown to a national footprint, while having intensely local impact. Selected as one of the *Dallas Business Journal*'s Outstanding Directors 2020, Betsy has spent her career in the nonprofit sector working to better the community. She and her wife, Sharon, enjoy traveling, wine tasting, cooking, and spending time with their little dog.

Shayla Partusch serves as the Vice President of Purchasing and Retail at Dickey's Barbecue Restaurants, Inc. She joined the Dickey's family in 2014 as a purchasing auditor and has since been deservingly promoted to her current role. Day to day, she oversees all supply chain distribution for every Dickey's location nationwide and handles all of Dickey's retail products in more than 3,000 grocery stores across the nation. Additionally, she leads Barbecue at Home by Dickey's, our direct to consumer brand. Her leadership, organization, and team attitude make Shayla a huge asset to the Dickey's family. Outside of Dickey's, Shayla enjoys golfing, playing cards with family and friends, and hanging out with her pup, Benji.

Jelena Frian, Carissa De Santis, Maja Perušić, Aaron Brewer, and Laura Rea in Croatia

Maja Perušić has been the Big Data Architect for Dickey's Barbecue Restaurants, Inc., for the past six years. When she's not working on data processing, you can find her reporting on and managing our BI Team. In partnership with Laura Rea Dickey, she has been able to lead a team in the creation of a data warehouse, based only on Aloha POS, and switched from Transweb to Yellowfin, based Smoke Stack, and has since worked with Spark POS and 3PV and introduced PBI-based Smoke Stack. She is passionate about data and believes every piece of information can be valuable. When Maja isn't working on pulling all of the data, she enjoys quiet days of painting and not-so-quiet board game evenings. Maja's hobbies allow her a quick recharge, which is the key to her success.

Croatia Development Team

Kristin Peterson joined Dickey's Barbecue Restaurants, Inc., as the Chief Marketing Officer after more than seventeen years developing omni-channel campaigns for national and international brands at the country's largest independent advertising agency. For the brand, she employs integration at every point of guest contact, including advertising, merchandising, digital, and public relations. Kristin's hobbies include running, gardening, and traveling.

Roland, Jr., with Renee Roozen

Tanya Pollock has the title of Travel Manager for Dickey's Barbecue but should probably be called magician extraordinaire. Whether it's skillfully handling personal business for the Dickey Family or juggling travel reservations for Dickey's field team of nearly forty road warriors, Tanya's organization and flexibility make her an asset to the brand and the people around her. Even though she spends her days booking travel for others, Tanya also loves traveling and a glass of good red wine.

Lauren, Aaron, Laura Rea, Renee, Carissa, and Betsy at ladies' leadership retreat

Jay Rooney holds the title of Chief Financial Officer at Dickey's Barbecue Restaurants, Inc. Joining the Dickey's team in 2017, Rooney oversees all Accounting, Finance, and Corporate Assets for the Dickey's brand, as well as all of our affiliate companies. Prior to joining our team at Dickey's, Jay had over twenty years of experience working in the finance field of the restaurant industry. His knowledge, experience, and patient demeanor are extremely beneficial to the success of our brand. When Jay isn't looking over budgets or crunching numbers, he enjoys traveling, hiking, rugby, and having adventures with his wife, Connie, daughters, Olivia and Natalie, and dogs, Coco and Roscoe.

Renee Roozen currently holds the position of Chief Administrative Officer at Dickey's Capital Group, Inc. Roozen has been working with the Dickey's family since 2015. In her very important role, Roozen is extremely involved in the "day to day" at the Dickey's Home Office, where she manages all human resources and legal functions. In addition, she oversees all office and cross-functional project management for Dickey's Barbecue Pit and all affiliate brands. Her brand famous "Woo-Hoo!!" is certain to give you a boost of energy. Outside of

Scott Nelson playing guitar on the patio of the original Dickey's location

the Dickey's walls, Renee enjoys spending time in the mountains of Colorado and/or on the lakes in Minnesota with her firefighter husband, Dan, and their mini-labradoodle, Coco.

Shannon Santos has been a valued member of the Dickey's Barbecue Restaurants, Inc., team since 2019, serving as our Communications Manager. She brings her positive attitude, impressive writing skills, and detailed organization to the table every day, making her a great asset to our brand. Shannon also never passes up the opportunity to assist with company events and party planning. Outside the Dickey's walls, she enjoys watching her

Renee and Roland, Jr., serving ice cream to the Home Office

Shannon Santos

Bernie Willcut and Laura Rea

Scott Nelson and Cody Monk

daughter, Harper, play tennis, live music, traveling, all things pizza, and sipping wine with her friends. When it comes to her core values, family and community top the list and, of course, barbecue.

Nick Schwabe is a longtime friend of Roland Dickey, Jr., from high school. He received his Bachelor of Science in Industrial Engineering from Louisiana Tech University and currently serves as CEO of Wycliff Douglas Foods, Inc., founded in 1998. He oversees the production facility located in Dallas, Texas, and works with clients by providing value-added personalized business solutions for their distribution needs. In addition to servicing clients around the world, he leads the production of Dickey's signature barbecue sauces, spices, and rubs, as well as private-label products for other restaurant companies. Nick is also

Central Bar crew: April Gann, Cameron Stapleton, Gary Stapleton, and Aaron Brewer

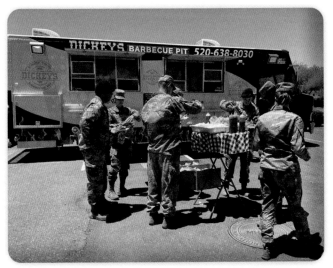

Dickey's Owner/Operator Darryl Weaver's food truck, feeding the National Guard

Ana Milhelic in Croatia

passionate about spending quality time with his family, boating, and enjoying a cold beer on the lake.

Gary Stapleton is the Honorary Mayor of Dickey's Central Bar and a successful businessman in Dallas. His passion for Texas-style barbecue began at an early age by frequently visiting Dickey's with his father in the 1950s. When he isn't greeting guests, he enjoys giving back to his local community by serving on the board of The Dickey Foundation, enjoys a good oyster, and loves spending time with his wife, Laura, and daughter, Cameron.

Sherri Stoel has been with Dickey's Barbecue Restaurants, Inc., for more than fourteen years and is the

Laura, Allison, and Mrs. Dickey

Dickey's Owner/Operators Chris and Mercedes Green with Mr. Dickey

heart and soul of Dickey's Accounting Department, where she is the Accounts Receivable Manager. She is passionate about working hard and prides herself on holding others accountable in the best interest of Dickey's Owner/Operators. Outside of work, Sherri enjoys visiting Canton, Texas, for a weekend of shopping at First Monday Trade Days. For those of you that have no idea, First Monday Trade Days is the World's Largest Flea Market. Largest or not, it is certainly Sherri's little piece of heaven.

Darryl Weaver knew he wanted to bring slow-smoked brisket to Tucson, Arizona, in 2015 after retiring from the United States Army. His passion to work the block and create genuine connections with his community is what sets him apart to be a successful Owner/Operator. When he isn't mentoring other Owner/Operators, you can oftentimes catch him bringing the 'cue to his guests around town in his Dickey's Food Truck.

#ShowUsYourCup

Maja, Tricia, and Carissa hard at work

Tricia Weir is the IT Systems Manager for Dickey's Barbecue Restaurants, Inc., and is responsible for Dickey's IT project management. Ms. Weir has over thirty years of food and beverage–industry experience from operations to menu design and development, inventory management, and systems management. Ms. Weir graduated from Michigan State University with a bachelor's degree in Food Systems Hospitality and Management. Tricia enjoys all things food, especially cooking, and is an avid outdoors enthusiast and cyclist.

Dickey's Owner/Operator Darryl Weaver and Pit Crew with Dickey's Food Truck

Josh Wise is a veteran in the restaurant and hospitality industry. His passion for pit-smoked barbecue started in 2018 when he opened his first location in Newark, Ohio. As one of our successful Owner/Operators, he has continued to expand outside of his Dickey's brick and mortar with a food truck to diversify and meet the needs of his guests through the pandemic. Josh credits his success and growth to developing and mentoring his own Pit Crews to better themselves and make the world a better place.

Wendy Williams, an Army Veteran, and her business partner, Karen Edwards, teamed up to bring Legit Texas Barbecue to Gulf Breeze, Florida, in 2018. These two women are passionate about barbecue and use their Dickey's Barbecue Pit restaurant to give back to first responders and the community. They are a powerhouse of community marketing and are often seen in their Dickey's-wrapped Hummer at community events, parades, and the beach.

Aaron Brewer, Mr. Dickey, Dickey's Owner/Operator Wendy Williams, and Laura Rea

INDEXES

CONTRIBUTOR INDEX

Mr. Dickey in King of Barbecue commercial

Team outing at the State Fair of Texas: Shannon Santos, Julie Moore, Greer Martin, and Carissa De Santis

CONTRIBUTOR INDEX

Nick Mitchell outside the original Dickey's location

Dickey's media coverage

Cinco de Mayo Trivia Winner, Simone Dominguez

CONTRIBUTOR INDEX

Dickey's Catering Commercial with Mr. Dickey and Joanna Windham parachuting

Family Business coverage

Dickey's female leadership group

RECIPE INDEX

RECIPE INDEX

RECIPE INDEX

RECIPE INDEX

RECIPE INDEX

RECIPE INDEX

RECIPE INDEX

RECIPE INDEX

DICKEY'S
RESTAURANT BRANDS

OUR GIFT TO YOU

We have something for everyone. Enjoy these family-favorite pit-smoked flavors from Dickey's Restaurant Brands.

APPLE   GOOGLE PLAY

15% OFF CATERING

Valid online or in the app only. Redeem at Dickeys.com with code 15COOK. One per order. Not valid with other offers or discounts.
Expires 12/31/2022

FREE SIDE WITH ANY SANDWICH

Valid online or in the app only. Redeem at Dickeys.com with code FREESIDECB. One per order. Not valid with other offers or discounts.
Expires 12/31/2022

$5 OFF $25 OR MORE

Valid online or in the Dickey's app only. Redeem with code COOK5. One per order. Not valid with other offers or discounts. Expires 12/31/2022

Dickeys.com | WingBoss.com | BigDealBurgerCo.com

20% OFF ANY BOX

Valid at BarbecueAtHome.com with code:

Cookbook-HDw4j2

One per order. Not valid with other offers or discounts. Expires 12/31/2022